INTRODUCING THE BIBLE

Introducing
the Bible

by

Neil S. Fujita

PAULIST PRESS　　*New York/Ramsey*

Acknowledgment
Excerpts from **The Documents of Vatican II**, *Abbott-Gallagher edition are reprinted with the permission of America Press, Inc., 106 West 56th Street, New York, New York 10019; copyright © 1966. All rights reserved.*

Library of Congress
Catalog Card Number: 81-80874

ISBN: 0-8091-2392-4

Published by Paulist Press
545 Island Road, Ramsey, N.J. 07446

Printed and bound in the United States of America

CONTENTS

v

Preface

Though numerous introductory books about the Bible have been published, very few are available which deal with both the Old and New Testaments together in a concise manner. Also, most Bible introductions are, by and large, either too technical or elementary in nature. This book intends to fill the existing vacuum; it presents a concentrated survey of the entire Bible explaining the origin, background, and general content as well as the theological ideas of basic significance in the individual biblical writings.

Needless to say, the very basic text of any biblical study is the Bible itself. Therefore, readers of the present book should follow the biblical text faithfully as they use this book as an aid.

I would like to express appreciation to the Rev. Lawrence Boadt, C.S.P., of the Paulist Press for his kind and helpful suggestions during the final preparation of the manuscript. Special gratitude is also due to Ms. Donna Blackstock, Br. Paul K. Hennessy, C.F.C., and the Rev. James Hicks, for they went over the entire manuscript and provided me with both corrections and valuable words of advice. Br. J. Richard DeMaria, C.F.C., and the Rev. Gerald Largo kindly read portions. I am beholden to Mr. George McKee for furnishing the maps. Finally, I would like to thank my wife, Eleanor, for her continual loving support.

Introduction

WHY THE BIBLE?

The Bible is perhaps the most widely read book in the world.[1] Historically, it has had a far-reaching impact on society and culture, particularly in the West. The book is of historical value, for it encompasses more than thirteen hundred years of the history of the ancient Near East. The Bible also has literary value, having inspired a multitude of great writers throughout many ages. It has moral value as well; its spiritual force has affected the lives of countless individuals, young and old. Undoubtedly, it constitutes an essential part of Western civilization.

The Bible is a literature of faith. Jews (with respect to the Hebrew Scripture) and Christians (with respect to both the Old and New Testaments) revere the Bible as the Word of God for its divinely inspired quality. It is a tangible source of authority for the members of these religious traditions. But what does divine inspiration of the Bible mean? And what kind of authority does the Bible exert? To put it simply, why do Jews and Christians use the Bible?

The authority of the Bible has often been supported by the claim that, being dictated by God word by word, the Bible as a whole is the Word of God, and thus entirely free from error, historical as well as theological.[2] This view, however, is untenable, since it confuses religious teachings with scientific

2

data and does not take seriously the time-bound nature of the Bible. Obviously some biblical stories cannot be taken literally (e.g., Noah's ark). The Bible is not, strictly speaking, a book of history, nor is it a science textbook. It is a religious book, and religious language is by nature symbolic. If a symbolic statement is taken factually, it not only obscures its message but it often becomes absurd as well. For example, the perplexity on the part of the Samaritan woman during the conversation with Jesus about the "living water" stems from her ignorance of the symbolic meaning of this "water," i.e., a spiritual gift which Jesus offers (Jn. 4:7–26).

The assertion that the Bible was "dictated" by God presents another problem: it assumes that the deity communicates with persons in much too mechanical a way. The Bible demonstrates two-way communication between God and people; God elicits human emotion, thought, and action, and people evoke God's response. The people of the Bible discovered and expressed the meaning and purpose of their lives in God. That which we have in the Bible is a series of faith expressions, that is, confession of faith in God.

Human beings are creatures of meaning. As we inquire into the meaning of our experiences, we participate in those experiences even more deeply. Meaning does not emerge from nothing, nor is it isolated. Meaning always arises in the historical and social context which people share. Therefore, meaning is by nature communal.

Religious meanings manifested in the Bible are also communal; the Bible is not simply a monopolized handiwork of certain religiously privileged individuals. It is a cumulative product of those believing communities (ancient Israel, Jews, and Christians), although certain persons did play significant roles in producing and preserving biblical writings.

Those believing communities were formed and developed during a span of more than one thousand years. Their common basis was their awareness of the same God, who communicated with them through their consciousness. The ultimate locus of divine revelation was the deeper realm of the human mind. Revelation preceded the composition of the biblical writings. The inspirational nature of the Bible, therefore, should be viewed in the light of such a communal and historical context. The Bible did not fall from heaven suddenly into human hands!

Why is the biblical confession of faith so important to people today? In what sense are the Old and New Testaments an authoritative norm for Christians? The answer is that both Testaments provide Christians with a fundamental pattern of faith.[3] The Bible furnishes the very basic source of knowledge concerning God and Jesus Christ, and it also generates faith in this God, which steers the life and community of believers. Christians are the ones who elect to follow this pattern in their lives. As such the Bible is a basis of teachings of the Christian community, the Church. Consequently, both the Old and New Testaments constitute a vital source of identity for Christians just as the Hebrew Scripture does for Jews.

HOW WE STUDY THE BIBLE

If the Bible is of such significance, how then do we approach it? It is not always an easy task to discover and actualize the exact pattern of biblical faith. In order to carry out a proper interpretation of the Bible, we should consider the following three aspects of basic importance.

1. Critical Study of the Bible

The Bible is a literary deposit of Near Eastern antiquity, which requires an intensive and extensive study of the biblical text and its background with the help of all available modern research in areas of archaeology, history, philology, literature, and comparative religions, as well as theology. In fact, the literary genre of the Bible presents great diversity; there are laws, history, genealogies, legends, folk tales, myths, poetry, and so forth, all of which arose from different times and situations. In order to investigate such literary and historical complexity, modern scholars have employed several methods of interpreting the biblical texts.

The biblical text should be examined carefully in an attempt to recover its original form as nearly as possible. Such a scholarly endeavor is called *textual criticism*. To this end, not only a precise scrutiny of the present Old Testament text in Hebrew and Aramaic (a cognate of Hebrew used in portions of Daniel and Ezra) and the Greek New Testament text is required, but also a scrupulous comparison of those texts with other extant ancient manuscripts and translations (Greek, Syriac, Latin, Coptic, etc.) is in order. For example, the biblical manuscripts from the caves near the Dead Sea (the first discovery of the Dead Sea Scrolls at Qumran was in 1947), which turned out to be the oldest textual evidence, have shed light on Old Testament textual criticism in a truly remarkable way.

The biblical text should be studied furthermore in respect to its origin and history, i.e., the authors and editors, historical occasions, aims, and sources of the composition. This academic process is called *literary-historical criticism*.

Modern scholars also have attempted to probe into the pre-literary state of the biblical material by singling out orally transmitted forms of tradition which underlie the written text. Since this method is concerned particularly with typical literary forms in relation to their function in concrete human life-situations, it is called *form criticism*. By locating and analyzing literary units in the biblical text according to their types or patterns of speech, form criticism strives to clarify the historical setting of these units so as to determine their intention and nature.

Since these literary units were historically transmitted, scholarly attention has also been directed to the historical process of transmission itself. This approach is termed *tradition-historical criticism*. This study intends also to trace the development of ideas and movements of the biblical people. For example, as a result of analyses of the sources, literary forms, and tradition-history, scholars have widely reached the conclusion that the initial five books of the Old Testament (traditionally called the Five Books of Moses) consist of writings of several different literary sources composed of numerous variegated literary units (e.g., sagas, myths, annals, legal materials, poems, and so on), each with its own origin and growth pattern, incorporated into the larger literary complex through manifold historical stages.

While form criticism is interested in the pre-literary stages of the biblical material, so-called *redaction criticism* appertains to a probe into the manner of usage, theological viewpoints, and intentions of the biblical writers who utilized oral tradition. In other words, it values the creativity and individuality of those writers (i.e., they were not just mechanical recorders but more or less intentional editors). For example, the four Gospels of the New Testament do not present homogeneous parallel stories of Jesus' life, but instead each of them offers its own unique literary and theological style in describing Jesus Christ. Thus redaction criticism is synthetic, while form criticism is intensely analytical; redaction criticism goes beyond the analysis of literary units and genre by examining their function within the larger literary scope.

In summary, critical study of the Bible is intended to construe the biblical text in its own setting in such a way that our understanding of the biblical message will be more accurate and mature, thereby averting arbitrary reading into the text of our own thoughts and whims.

2. Traditional Exposition of the Bible

Our approach to the Bible will be more sound if we give serious attention to various interpretations of the Bible tendered in the past, since meaning is always communal and historical. The Bible was born in and has been preserved by believing communities. For centuries, people have asked, "Who am I?" "Where am I going?" "Why do we have such problems?" "What does God mean to us?" Believers have found a basic source for answers to these questions in the Bible. And the God who communicated with the biblical people has continuously guided his believing community. Therefore, the insight and instruction which the believing community has provided will assist us in our understanding of the Bible. No interpreter is isolated from the cumulative results of past exposition, and no interpretation is separated from the environment from which it springs. This does not mean that the individuality of each interpreter is to be denied, for instead it is enriched.

3. Existential Understanding of the Bible

The third aspect of importance in biblical interpretation is maintaining sensitivity and wisdom concerning our own problems of today. Our serious search for answers to our contemporary predicament parallels the spiritual struggles of the biblical people. Only a sincere dialogue between today's perceptive mind and the Bible will result in a proper appreciation of the biblical messages, which has the possibility of leading us to the discovery of solutions to our problems.

A proper interpretation of the Bible will be carried out when these three approaches to the Bible are executed in a well-balanced way. Above all, of vital significance is openness on the part of the reader—openness to let the Bible speak for itself. Biblical interpretation may be, in a way, compared to appreciation of art and music in the sense that it transcends objective and cognitive understanding. Interpretative goals cannot be attained until one's soul resonates to the heart of the biblical authors.

CONTENTS OF THE BIBLE

1. The Canon of the Old Testament

The Old Testament, which the Christians inherited from the Jews and so named to collocate with the New Testament, is usually called the *Tanak* by Jews, which is an acronym derived from the names of its three literary groups: *Torah* (Law—the first five books), *Nebi'im* (historical and prophetical books), and *Kethubim* (poetry and wisdom literature).

Those three groups of writings attained official status ("canonization," i.e., the official acknowledgment of these books as authentic reflection of the faith of the believing community) as a result of a compilatory process over centuries. It was often maintained that the Torah attained its canonical status by 400 B.C. and Nebi'im by 200 B.C., but recently scholars insist that the two collections were joined at an early date, and then further expanded. They were thus shaped into normative form between 500 and 200 B.C. The section called Kethubim is considered to have become authoritative by the end of the first century A.D. At the rabbinic council at Jamnia (ca. A.D. 90), the Jewish canon took its fundamental form.

When the earlier Greek-speaking Christians appropriated the Tanak, they naturally used its Greek translation—the so-called *Septuagint.* The Septuagint was the product of rabbis in Alexandria, Egypt, during the last three centuries B.C., and it included several additional books which were written during the two hundred years before Christ. They are Tobit, Judith, Wisdom of Solomon, Ecclesiasticus, Baruch, 1, 2, 3 and 4 Maccabees, 1 Esdras, the Prayer of Manasseh, the addition to Daniel, and the addition to Esther. Ancient rabbis, following the Hebrew Palestinian Scripture, did not deem these later writings equal to the canonical literature.

Roman Catholics have retained basically the Alexandrian Scripture (except for 3 and 4 Maccabees, 1 Esdras, and the Prayer of Manasseh), and designate those additional books as "deutero-canonical" (i.e., books which were later added to the canon). Protestants decided at the time of the Reformation to accept the books of the original Hebrew Scripture as their canon, and considered those additional books as being unequal to the canonical books, yet "useful and good for reading" (Luther), by calling them the "Apocrypha" (i.e., "hidden" or withdrawn from common use).

The Books of the Old Testament

Torah—Genesis, Exodus, Leviticus, Numbers, Deuteronomy

Historical Books—Joshua, Judges, Ruth, 1 and 2 Samuel, 1 and 2 Kings, 1 and 2 Chronicles, Ezra, Nehemiah, Tobit, Judith, Esther, 1 and 2 Maccabees

Prophetical Books—Isaiah, Jeremiah, Baruch, Ezekiel, Daniel, Joel, Amos, Hosea, Obadiah, Jonah, Micah, Nahum, Habakkuk, Zephaniah, Haggai, Zechariah, Malachi

Poetry and Wisdom—Job, Psalms, Proverbs, Ecclesiastes, Song of Solomon, Lamentations, Ecclesiasticus, Wisdom of Solomon

2. The Canon of the New Testament

The canonization of the New Testament was also a long and gradual process. In fact, there is no clear evidence of the existence of a universally accepted canon during the first three centuries A.D. Many of Paul's letters seemingly attained an authoritative status among Christians by the early second century. The four Gospels apparently became a closed collection as early as the second century, whereas James, Jude, 2 Peter, 2 and 3 John, and Revelation were often debated as to their "genuineness" as late as the early fourth century. Basically, the ancient Church intended to canonize the writings which it considered to have originated from the apostles.

In the fourth century, as the Christian Church entrenched itself in Europe after the conversion of the Roman emperor Constantine (A.D. 312), the time was ripe for the establishment of the New Testament canon to aid in further consolidating Christendom. The Western Christians accepted all twenty-seven books of the present canon at a council in Hippo (A.D. 393) and again at the Third Council of Carthage (A.D. 397 and 419). The Roman Catholic canon received its final definition at the Council of Trent (A.D. 1545-1563). Since the Reformation in the sixteenth century, Protestants have been using all twenty-seven books as the New Testament canon. As far as the Eastern Orthodox Christians are concerned, their canon has not been clearly defined.[4]

All Orthodox, Catholic, and Protestant churches now commonly endorse the Revised Standard Version, a revised edition of the older English translation called the King James Version of 1611 (the Old Testament section in 1952 and the New Testament section in 1946). All the quotations used by this author in this book are from the Revised Standard Version. Other English translations of the Bible which have been published since 1960 and are now widely circulated are: the

Jerusalem Bible (Catholic, 1966), the New English Bible (jointly, British Catholic and Protestant, 1970), the New American Bible (Catholic, 1970), the Good News Bible (Protestant, 1976), the New International Version of the Bible (Protestant, 1978), and the New Jewish Publication Society translation (the Torah in 1963 and the Prophets in 1978).

The Books of the New Testament
   Gospels—Matthew, Mark, Luke, John
   Letters attributed to Paul—Romans, 1 and 2 Corinthians, Galatians, Ephesians, Philippians, Colossians, 1 and 2 Thessalonians, 1 and 2 Timothy, Titus, Philemon
   Catholic Letters—James, 1 and 2 Peter, 1, 2, 3 John, Jude
   Other Writings—Acts, Hebrews, Revelation

QUESTIONS FOR DISCUSSION

1. What is meant by the "canonization" of the Bible?

2. Why has the Bible been revered by Christians?

3. Can the view regarding the Bible as inerrant be tenable? What evidence pertinent to this question does the Bible itself yield?

4. Explain various ways of interpreting biblical passages.

5. Why does the Church need the Bible today?

6. Have you ever felt strongly that certain particular biblical passages were important to you on some specific occasion? Reflect upon such experiences analytically—when, why, and how.

7. Is the Bible a kind of literature different from other writings?

8. How significant is the Bible in today's society?

Part I

THE OLD TESTAMENT

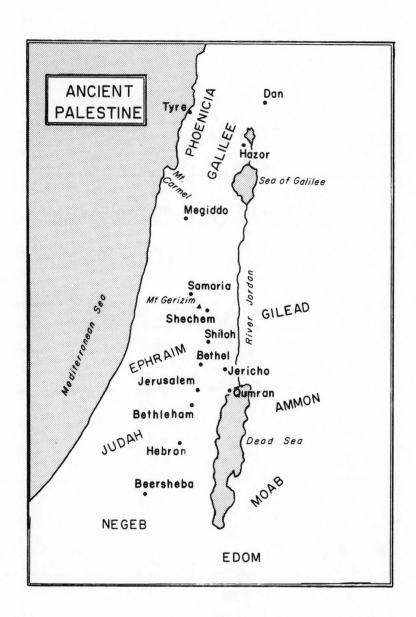

ANCIENT PALESTINE

PHOENICIA
GALILEE
Dan
Tyre
Hazor
Mt. Carmel
Sea of Galilee
Megiddo
Samaria
Mt Gerizim
Shechem
River Jordan
GILEAD
Shiloh
EPHRAIM
Bethel
Jericho
Jerusalem
Qumran
AMMON
Bethleham
Mediterranean Sea
Dead Sea
JUDAH
Hebron
Beersheba
MOAB
NEGEB
EDOM

12

Chapter One

THE TETRATEUCH

1. FORMATION OF THE TETRATEUCH

The Tetrateuch refers to the initial four books of the Old Testament (Genesis, Exodus, Leviticus, Numbers). It is appropriate to discuss them together as one literary set because they consist of common literary sources. These sources, though originally distinct, are narrative strands woven together and running throughout the Tetrateuch. They contain a considerable diversity of historical and geographical references, legal statements, literary styles, and theological views. For example, according to Exodus 3 and 6:2, God revealed his name, Yahweh, for the first time to Moses, while Genesis 4:26 records that the name had been known by people long before Moses. Such great complexities found in the Tetrateuch lead us to assume that there was, instead of a single author like Moses, a cumulative growth of divergent sources through a long period of time.

Scholars' analysis of the Tetrateuch have resulted in a now universally accepted conclusion that the following three major literary sources can be detected: the Yahwist, the Elohist, and the Priestly sources.

The Yahwist source, the oldest of these three, is so named by scholars for its consistent use of the divine name, Yahweh.

GROWTH OF PENTATEUCHAL SOURCES (JEDP)

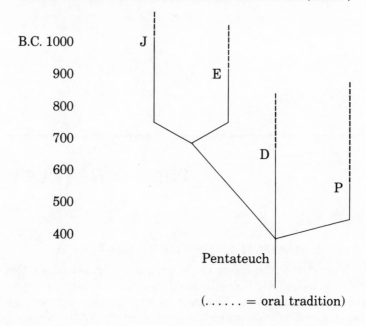

(. . . . . = oral tradition)

This source—or the person(s) responsible for producing it—is often designated by the letter J, the initial of Jahwe (so spelled by German pioneers in this academic field). The letter J also stands for "Judah" because the source has an apparent association with that southern tribe. The J source was composed most likely in the tenth century B.C., a time which marked the heyday of Israel, when the country, under the reign of David and Solomon, enjoyed its greatest political and social stability, economic expansion, and cultural enlightenment. The J author collected and narrated earlier traditions which had been orally transmitted up until that time. It included the stories of primordial myths, the patriarchs, Israel's deliverance from Egypt, her sojourn through the Sinai wilderness, and her settlement in the promised land, Canaan. All of these, accord-

GENERAL LOCATION OF PENTATEUCHAL SOURCES

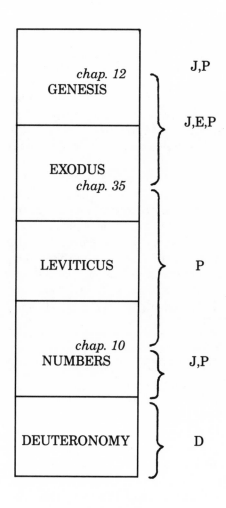

ing to J, gave witness to genuine experiences of God. J thus provided the Tetrateuch with a literary framework.

The Elohist source (E), so named because of its use of the Hebrew word for God (Elohim) and also because of its presumable origin in Ephraim, a territory north of Jerusalem, is dated from the ninth century B.C. (at which time the height of Israel's prosperity had passed and the country was divided into two states: Judah in the south and Israel in the north). The content of the E source, though fragmentary, runs parallel to that of J (from Abraham to the settlement) and betrays the influence of the prophets. Through the redactional process, J and E were combined sometime during the seventh century B.C.—so closely conflated together that it is often too arduous a task to isolate one from the other.

The Priestly source (P), which is characterized by its special interest in matters germane to the priesthood and cult, perhaps was compiled by priestly circles in exile in Babylon following the fall of Jerusalem in 587 B.C. The P source is found scattered all through the Tetrateuch from Genesis 1 (creation narrative) to the end of Numbers (Moses' death), thereby greatly enriching the JE tradition. The Tetrateuchal aggregation reached its final (i.e., present) form by approximately 400 B.C.

2. PRIMORDIAL NARRATIVES (GENESIS 1–11)

This section includes the narratives of creation (1–2), the Garden of Eden (3), Cain and Abel (4), Noah (6–9), and the tower of Babel (11), as well as the genealogies (5, 10, 11). These narrative units are arranged genealogically, but they are not history in the modern sense of the word. Their genealogical concern is, in reality, to illumine the fundamental meaning and purpose of human life. Hence it is utterly pointless to dispute the scientific compatibility of the creation accounts or to search for the original site of the garden. The literary genre of almost all of these narratives is myth.

Myths are not non-scientific tales conjured up by primitive minds, but are instead a legitimate and significant literary vehicle for unfolding the meaning of human existence, the universe, as well as the deities. The language of myths is by nature symbolic, which is an essential characteristic of religious language. Therefore, it cannot be judged verifiably true or false; it is rather to be understood without cognitive analysis as the way things are, or can be, or ought to be. It represents a people's fundamental understanding of themselves (a familiar modern myth might be the so-called American dream). There is thus a unique correlation between the claim of myths and the factual data of history. Certain historical data are sometimes "mythified" so as to provide them with interpretation or meaning. Characteristically, religious literature often presents such myths.

Creation Accounts

The creation myth consists of two different versions: one by P (1:1–2:4a) and the other by J (2:4b–25). They differ from each other in many respects. The former, written in the rueful situation of the Babylonian exile, depicts the divine creation of the cosmos in a highly orderly and stylized fashion. This epic provides no explanation as to how the world came to exist; the idea of creation being formed out of nothing is not mentioned here. Instead, the writer describes the creation as a transformation from chaos to cosmos (orderly world). By presenting the transformation in a chronological sequence, the idea is underscored that this creative change is an on-going process—a process from the primordial stage ("the first day") to the culmination of this dynamic history (the cosmic sabbath, "the seventh day"). God's creativity is operative all through this process, yet God as the transcendent Creator, unlike the Babylonian polytheistic gods, is not identified with any natural forces.

This unique creation theology of P seems to have had particular relevance in the exilic condition in which the author and his compatriots found themselves; they had lost everything when the country fell, and as exiles there was no hope for them in the conqueror's land—utter chaos. In this devastating situation, P proclaimed emphatically that alive and present with these hopeless people was the creative God who would transform chaos to cosmos. In this selfsame God, P declared, should true hope repose. (Note, he repeated the sentence, "It was good," in vv. 3, 10, 18, 21, 25, 31.) In brief, the message of Genesis 1 is that God's creative presence is the ultimate source of hope.

In contrast to P, J's narrative, written in the prosperous age of the tenth century B.C., has its focus on the purpose of man's existence (Adam is not a personal name but a generic noun for man). Adam is to take care of the world in which he is placed (2:15). He is part of nature ("dust-made" in v. 7), yet has a unique responsibility to actualize God-given potentialities not only within himself but also within the world. He and his wife are to be good stewards (vv. 19f.); their labor is blessed and their world joyful ("Eden" means pleasure). For this purpose, freedom and intelligence are endowed uniquely to them.

However, J says, they misuse this freedom. That is the theme of the garden story (chapter 3). Their eating of the forbidden fruit symbolizes an audacious claim of human autonomy in opposition to God's sovereignty, which results in their expulsion from the garden, i.e., a decisive severance of relationship ("death" in v. 3) between God and the people (here the meaning of "death" is put in question, for Adam and Eve did not physically die, though it says in 2:17, "In the day that you eat of it you shall die").

And he [Adam] said, "I heard the sound of thee in the garden, and I was afraid, because I was naked; and I hid myself " (3:10).
To the woman he [God] said,
"I will multiply your pain in childbearing;
in pain you shall bring forth your children,
yet your desire shall be for your husband,
and he shall rule over you" (3:16).

And to Adam he [God] said,
"Because you listened to the voice of your wife,

and have eaten of the tree of which I commanded
    you,
'You shall not eat of it,'
cursed is the ground because of you;
in toil you shall eat of it all the days of your life;
thorns and thistles it shall bring forth to you;
and you shall eat the plants of the field.
In the sweat of your face you shall eat bread
till you return to the ground,
for out of it you were taken;
you are dust, and to dust you shall return" (3:17–
    19).

Notice that these few verses encompass problems concerning very basic aspects of human life: sexuality, work, birth, death, human relationship, and nature. In this "death" state, sexuality is shadowed by shame, labor by suffering, procreation by pain, and human relationship by aggression and enmity. The human misuse of freedom through the claiming of autonomy brings disastrous transformation to the whole of human life.

Notice also that the human tragedy affects nature as well. Here again the idea is that the people belong to nature with vital responsibilities to nature. Ecological concern is not just a twentieth century question. The biblical writer of old has already stressed human responsibility and solidarity with nature; people cannot really take care of themselves unless they also do justice to their environment. The oft-claimed assertion that Western technological aggressiveness stems partly from the biblical sanction to "have dominion over" creatures (Gen. 1:28) is gratuitous, for this "aggressiveness" is a recent phenomenon; moreover, not every follower of the Bible has adhered to this interpretation or pursued its path.

Genesis 3 thus describes a collapse of the wholeness of the world. This "un-whole-some" state is sin, though the word "sin" does not occur in this particular chapter. It is an arbitrary claim of human autonomy which radically denies God's sovereignty. It is also a source of pain and suffering and is a hindrance to the actualization of God-given potentialities. It is, therefore, comparable to death.

This "death" is followed by another death in the next chapter: Cain kills his brother—a severance of human relationship. Contrary to Cain's words, we are supposed to be our "brother's keeper" (4:9). As our author views it, the severance of relationship between God and people causes the severance of human relationship, and thus sin prevails.

Flood Narrative

The flood narrative depicts the sinful state of man in a universal dimension. The consequence is God's judgment upon the world, excepting the family of the righteous man Noah and his pairs of "every living thing of all flesh" (6:19). Noah is an ancient legendary figure of a righteous man attested to by Near Eastern documents of antiquity. In Ezekiel 14:14, Noah is mentioned alongside Job and Daniel as an exemplary upright person. Stories connected with an enormous flood are also ancient and universal. The so-called Gilgamesh Epic from Babylonia presents an interesting parallel to the biblical flood narrative. Scholars are of the opinion that both of these flood stories came from an even older Sumerian legend (the second millennium B.C.). However, in contrast to the clear monotheistic stance of the biblical story, the Babylonian legend exhibits an extremely crude polytheistic perception. Moreover, the former demonstrates a highly ethical and religious quality by driving home the message of divine judgment, while the latter provides no real reason behind the flood, suggesting only that it resulted from an arbitrary vote of gods.

After the flood is over, God establishes a covenant with Noah, pledging a re-creation of the world. This Noahic covenant narrative (9:1–17) belongs to the Priestly source. As we have observed in the message of hope of the Priestly theologian in Genesis 1, here again we encounter the same theme. The flood seems to symbolize the chaotic condition of exile, but God provides the people with hope by creating the cosmos out of chaos. The covenant is a legal metaphor of this new relationship between God and the world through the mediatorship of Noah.

Story of the Tower of Babel

The story of the tower of Babel (11:1–9) is the last of the primordial narratives by the Yahwist. This story can be related to the temple towers (ziggurats) of ancient Mesopotamia. These massive towers, several hundred feet tall of brick and stone, were used for worship. The Yahwist writer sees in these monuments a fitting symbol of human arrogance, intruding into the divine realm, which is the cause of doom—the confusion of language and severe breakdown of communication. Thus the primordial narrative closes with a catastrophic note, but it anticipates a new beginning—God's initiative of salvation through the patriarchs.

3. PATRIARCHAL NARRATIVES (GENESIS 12–50)

Throughout the initial eleven chapters of Genesis, human sin continues to aggregate, yet God's salvific intention invariably overwhelms it and culminates in his promise to Abraham (12:1–3). God reveals his intention that he will bless Abraham and will make out of him "a great nation," so that "all the families of the earth" may participate in a divine blessing through him. God's plan for the salvation of mankind through Abraham is of central significance in the Yahwist message. He addresses this message to Israel during a prosperous age (the tenth century B.C.) in order to remind them of God's faithfulness in keeping his promise which brought to them much felicity, and also to teach them their responsibility to other nations. To achieve his goal, the Yahwist says, God works through mediators, and Abraham responds to the call for this mission. Thus the stories of the patriarchs commence.

The patriarchal narratives consist of three originally independent cycles: the story of Abraham-Isaac (12–26), Jacob-Esau (27–36), and Joseph (37–50). These are not histories but are to be classified as sagas. It is extremely difficult to reconstruct the life and thought of the patriarchs. But thanks to historical and archaeological research (particularly the discovery and translation of the tablets from Mari in Mesopotamia), it seems safe to assume that these patriarchs were West-Semitic pastoral nomads of the middle-bronze age (ca. 20th-18th centuries B.C.). The nucleus of the traditions preserved in these sagas may be traced back to that period.[1] However, our narratives are a final product of theological redactions. These theological ideas are our main concern.

Abraham-Isaac Cycle

The central theme of the Abraham-Isaac cycle is faith in God's promise; God will bless Abraham (12:1–3), give him a son (17:15–21; 18:10), increase his descendants (13:16, etc.), and grant him the land to settle (15:7–21, etc.). With this faith, Abraham migrates from Mesopotamia to Canaan, becomes a sojourner in Egypt due to a famine, begets Isaac despite his and his wife's old age, and passes God's test (the dramatic story in 22:1–14 in which the father nearly sacrifices the son). The cycle closes with the account of Isaac's marriage with Rebekah, a girl from his ancestral homeland in Mesopotamia. The theme of God's promise of blessing to Abraham (12:1–3) is, in fact, repeatedly stated in this cycle (12:7; 13:14–17; 15:1–21; 17:1–8, 16, 19–21; 18:18–19; 22:16–18; 24:7, 35).

To have faith in God's promise means being willing to commit oneself to the God who alone provides firm ground for hope and expectations. Hope for a future is a uniquely human ability. For a people without faith, the future is simply an unknown realm. But for people with faith, it is something open and real in which they anticipate a growth in the meaning of their existence.

Abraham represents a figure living this life with faith in God's promise. He accepts God's word in solemn faith, and it is this faith which places him in a proper relationship with God (15:6). The biblical author tells us that he has become "the father of a multitude of nations" (17:4), who, as such, plays the role of mediator between God and the people (12:3; 18:22–33). In fact, Abraham occupies a dominant place in the Bible as a model of one with great faith. For example, he is called God's "friend" (Is. 41:8), and Paul perceives Christians as the true spiritual heirs of Abraham (Rom. 4; Gal. 3).

Jacob-Esau Cycle

In the Jacob-Esau cycle, we are able to observe a typical case of a man who mistakes earthly success for ultimate happiness, yet is not abandoned by God and later becomes an heir of the tradition of faith. This man is Jacob, who shrewdly tricks his twin but first-born brother, Esau, out of his birthright and the father's ultimate blessing. Jacob's crafty act to gain earthly success, however, drives him into a further struggle. Out of fear of Esau, he goes for refuge to Laban, his uncle, for whom he has to devote long and hard work. In a period of despair, Jacob hears God reiterate the promise given to Abraham (28:13–15). Jacob's initial reaction reveals a striking irony in the man's life: "Surely the Lord is in this place, and I did not know it" (v. 16). It is indeed in the midst of self-inflicted despondency that a man, without anticipation, encounters God who, in reality, has been there awaiting him in order to give him hope for the future. After years of labor, Jacob marries, obtains property, and returns home. The narrator (J) tells us that later Jacob becomes the father of the twelve tribes of Israel. Indeed, God's blessing is the central theme of the Jacob-Esau narrative.[2]

Joseph Story

The Joseph story was originally an independent and integral literary entity, which the Yahwist compiler incorporated into the whole scheme of his patriarchal narratives. Joseph shows an interesting contrast to Jacob. In Jacob's case, the failure of his craftiness eventuates in an encounter with God, while in Joseph's case a vicious intrigue results in the victim's (Joseph's) success. But in both, God's way develops in a manner diametrically opposite to human expectation.

Joseph is sold by his brothers, yet in overcoming recurring misfortune by use of his talents and diligence, he prospers in Egypt. When a famine strikes Canaan, the brothers have to come and beg for food from Joseph although they do not recognize him as their own brother. In the end, he forgives them and is united even with his father Jacob, who thought that his lost son was dead. The story concludes with this message:

> As for you, you meant evil against me; but God meant
> it for good, to bring it about that many people should
> be kept alive, as they are today (50:20).

Throughout these stories of the patriarchs a picture clearly emerges. In this life people struggle, sometimes driven by an insatiable thirst for success and when not successful thus sinking deeply into despair or at other times striving toward high ideals and piety, and being elevated aloft in joy and happiness. God is there to meet people in both situations, confronting them in the sorrowful abyss as well as in the height of glory. He is to them all the ultimate ground of the meaning of life and the source of hope. The patriarchal narratives beautifully paint this drama of the encounter between God and people. And so now that the children of Jacob are assembled in Egypt, a new story is about to commence: the exodus.

4. THE EXODUS AND THE WANDERING IN THE WILDERNESS

Hebrews in Egypt

The Tetrateuchal writers assumed that the twelve sons of Jacob sojourning in Egypt were the founding fathers of the twelve tribes of Israel. But historical probability tends to indicate that they were no more than eponyms, and that Israel's twelve-tribal system did not come into existence until after the exodus event, its formation resulting from a long process of gradual growth.

Nonetheless, it is generally assumed that a Semitic group called the Hebrews was in Egypt. It has often been mentioned that these Hebrews may be identified with the people referred to by the name *Apiru* or *Habiru* in a wide range of documents of Egypt, Mesopotamia, and Syria from the eighteenth down to the fourteenth century B.C. But a direct identification is untenable, for the patriarchs seem to have been rather peaceful, pastoral nomads, while the *Apiru* were roaming all over those areas (concentrating mainly on the fringes of the desert) and were, by and large, groups of plunderers. Besides, despite an apparent phonetic resemblance between *Habiru* and Hebrew, controversial etymological evidence weakens this association. It is nonetheless not impossible to assume some social contact between the two peoples. Not only did such a well-known movement of the West-Semitic people as the *Apiru* and the Hyksos (who invaded and established power in the eastern Nile Delta in the 18th century B.C.) take place, but also migration due to famine occurred frequently (cf. Gen. 12:10; 26:1; 47:4). In fact, some personal names which appear in biblical stories of the exodus are ancient Egyptian names: Moses, Phinehas, Hophni, Merari, etc. These facts seemingly indicate that the direct ancestors of Israel were actually in Egypt.

However, no outside evidence is available as far as the enslavement and subsequent flight of the Hebrews are concerned. Yet it is again reasonable to assume the historicity of these events, even though the biblical stories pertinent to them are literary and theological embellishments. First of all, it is rather inconceivable that later Israelites excogitated such a shameful past. In fact, the memory of their deliverance later constituted a kernel of Israel's tradition.

Second, Exodus 11:1 records that the Hebrew slaves were forced to build for the pharaoh the "store-cities, Pithom and Raameses." Pithom has been identified with Tell el-Makhutah in the eastern part of the delta and is called Succoth in the Old Testament. Archaeological exploration has brought to light a large granite statue of Raameses II and huge storage places. The identification of Raameses is in dispute. If it was Per-Raameses, the city was founded by his father Sethos I and completed by the son, Raameses II. If this was the case, the forced labor must have occurred in the second half of the thirteenth century B.C.

Third, the earliest known reference to Israel comes from the successor of Raameses II, Merneptah, who left a stele to commemorate his victorious campaign; it bears the inscription: "The people of Israel is destroyed, it has no offspring." This monument is dated 1230 B.C. For these three major reasons, we may conclude that the Hebrews suffered under Raameses II from the hard labor of enslavement, which resulted in their flight, and that they eventually succeeded in settling down in Canaan by 1230 B.C.

The Exodus

The biblical tradition tells us that Moses was born a Hebrew but was abandoned because of the pharaoh's order to kill Hebrew male infants. A fortuitous fate, however, provided

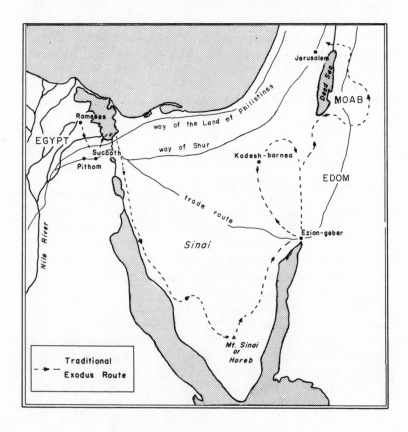

that he was raised with the help of the pharaoh's daughter. A pattern such as this in the formation of a leader's life is found rather widely in ancient stories, reminding us of the intriguing developments in the patriarchal stories. The theological motif which we have observed in the preceding section seems to rebound here: human evil intends to harm a hero, but God means it for good (Gen. 50:20).

According to the Exodus story, upon killing an Egyptian, Moses takes refuge among the Midianites (also called Kenites), pastoral nomads in Sinai and Arabia, and he becomes a son-in-law of the tribal chief, Jethro (also called Reuel or Hobab). At this time of crisis, God speaks to him (Ex. 3–4). This pattern resembles events in Jacob's life (Gen. 28); in fact, several themes are in common in both cases: (1) God's identity as the God of the patriarchs; (2) God's presence with his people— his salvific intention; (3) God's promise of the land and posterity.

Revelation of God's Name

In the exodus story, however, a significant new development is marked: the revelation of God's name, Yahweh, at Mount Sinai (also called Horeb). God tells Moses that his name is "I am who I am." The divine name "Yahweh" in the Old Testament is the Hebrew word meaning "he is" or "he causes." It transfers God's first person singular "I am" to the third person singular "he is," referring to God from a human point of view. "Yahweh" can be rendered in the future tense and also in the causative (i.e., "he will cause."). Despite various attempts by scholars, the real meaning of this divine name cannot be determined conclusively. God remains a mystery to people, yet we may be justified in asserting that his name indicates God's presence, integrity, and creativity.

God's revelation of his name is of vital significance as he sends Moses to rescue his people. In the ancient world, a name embodied its essence. Therefore, for example, the third commandment of the Decalogue says, "You shall not take the name of the Lord your God in vain," i.e., one should not abuse God himself. Likewise Christians pray in the name of Jesus

Christ. The revelation of the divine name thus signifies the fact that God himself resides with Moses and his people in the midst of suffering. God is not some sort of philosophical notion nor simply a product of human emotion but one who listens to human outcry and is willing to be involved in historical reality. Such divine commitment urges the terrified Moses to bravely confront the powerful oppressor, demanding, "Let my people go!" As in the case of the patriarchs, here, too, God works through a human medium.

Liberation

The accounts in Exodus 5–15 do not furnish us with an objective photographic presentation of the sequence of the exodus events, but instead bear witness to the salvific intention of God. It is thus impossible to reconstruct what actually happened. We could assume it more probable that the Hebrew slaves escaped from Egypt in waves of small groups, a core of which was led by Moses. It is improbable that after the ten plagues "600,000 men on foot besides women and children" with many domestic animals left at the urging of the Egyptians (Ex. 12:33–38). In fact, there is a hint of what happened in Exodus 14:5: "When the king of Egypt was told that the people had fled . . ." At any rate, we are told that they succeeded in fleeing from the pursuing Egyptian troops by crossing the Sea of Reed (not Red Sea). It is again beyond our reach to determine exactly where and how they traversed a body of water. The point of fundamental significance is that this event constituted specifically a religious experience—an experience of liberation: slaves became free men!

Freedom signifies availability of choice; the more available choices there are, the freer one feels. Under enslavement, people are deprived of this vitally unique human endowment—freedom. This results in a dehumanization, which is perhaps the worst brutality imaginable. Furthermore, when one is able to choose, one is able to search for relevant meaning. Thus, liberation means an acquisition of meaningfulness. As a noted psychiatrist, Viktor Frankl, who himself survived the Nazi holocaust, tells us, those who persisted in searching for meaning could remain human and in fact even endure through the intolerable condition of the death camp.[3] By searching for meaning, one is choosing oneself.

The ancient people of Israel, risking their lives by choosing to obey the God who sent Moses, found meaning in their lives. Yet, in the wilderness where their struggle continued and their perplexity deepened, they wondered: Is this life worth living? Is God with us? (Ex. 17:7) Moses confronted the people with the fundamental alternative: their freedom in the wilderness or the "fleshpots" of bondage in Egypt (Ex. 16). The former would promise a future, while the latter would effect dehumanization.

The liberation experience through the exodus event thus constituted an axiom of Israel's religious tradition where God was often referred to as the "God who led us out of the house of bondage" (Ex. 20:2; Deut. 5:6, etc.). The feast of Passover, celebrated by Jews over the centuries even to this day, has the intent of allowing the celebrants to existentially participate in the ancient experience of that liberation through liturgy. Such a process of religious experience in the Jewish ceremony is identical to the Christian celebration of the Eucharist (based on the last Passover meal before the crucifixion) which commemorates the sacrifice of Jesus Christ. In the liturgical context, temporal sequence loses its validity; past becomes present and present future, and vice versa.

The Sinai Covenant

The Sinai wilderness was a place of Israel's continuing struggle, yet it was a locus for their encounter with God as well. According to the biblical tradition, this latter experience occurred in the area centered in Mount Sinai (the location of which is uncertain, though it has been traditionally identified with Jebel Musa in the southern Sinai peninsula) and an oasis, Kadesh-Barnea (*kadesh* means holy in Hebrew, i.e., there was a sanctuary there). The Israelites encamped at this oasis area for a lengthy period. During this period of time, they formed themselves into one nation with a common faith in Yahweh. The climax of this process was the establishment of a covenant—a legal form in which the living relationship between Israel and Yahweh was actualized. A covenantal formula: "I shall be your God and you shall be my people" summarily expressed that fact.

As evidenced by a good number of parallels from the ancient Near Eastern world (e.g., the Hittite covenant treaty), covenant-making essentially involves legal stipulations. Exactly so is the case with the biblical section pertaining to the Sinai experience. The law provides the people of Yahweh with guidance for their lives; it is a practical demonstration of his will. There is a huge bulk of legal material in this section, which is dominated by the Priestly source (Ex. 25–31; 35–40; the entire Leviticus; Num. 5–10). This fact does not necessarily mean that all of these laws belong to the exilic period, but, as scholars observed, they, in fact, preserve many ancient traditions.

A cornerstone of the legal heritage of Israel is the well-known Decalogue (Ten Commandments) recorded in Exodus 20 (E) and Deuteronomy 5. These two passages contain some variant texts. A reconstructed version is as follows:

1. You shall have no other gods besides me.
2. You shall not make yourself a graven image.
3. You shall not invoke the name of Yahweh your God in vain.
4. Remember the sabbath day, to keep it holy.
5. Honor your father and your mother.
6. You shall not kill.
7. You shall not commit adultery.
8. You shall not steal.
9. You shall not bear false witness against your neighbor.
10. You shall not covet your neighbor's house.

Although our Decalogue, too, is a result of a long series of redaction, its nucleus may well go back to the Mosaic time. Such prohibition lists were, in fact, not uncommon in the ancient Near East (an example is the Egyptian "Book of the Dead," chapter 125). Some scholars believe that perhaps Moses himself compiled the list and his priestly successors preserved it. Israel's religion can be characterized as eminently ethical even in a time as ancient as its inchoate period in the wilderness.

Monotheism

In addition to its highly ethical nature, Israel's faith at Moses' time (the so-called Mosaic faith) possesses another important characteristic, i.e., the belief in one God. This, in fact, is its most striking quality. The once-alleged influence of Pharaoh Akhenaton's exclusive devotion to the sun-god, Aton, in the fourteenth century B.C. is untenable since it is not at all a genuine monotheism (for example, Pharaoh himself is considered divine). Also dubious is the so-called Kenite theory which traces the origin of the worship of Yahweh to Jethro, Moses' father-in-law.

However, it should be noted that the Mosaic faith cannot be called a monotheism in a strict sense of the term either, since the biblical tradition from this early stage shows no explicit evidence of a denial of other deities. In fact, Joshua, the successor of Moses, demands that the Israelites choose which deity to serve, Yahweh or the gods of Mesopotamia and Egypt (Jos. 24; cf. also Jgs. 11:24; 1 Sam. 26:19). The first commandment forbids Israel to worship gods other than Yahweh, but falls short of actually rejecting the existence of other gods. Nor does the well-known passage in Deuteronomy 6:4 ("Hear, O Israel, the Lord your God is one Lord") exclude the existence of other deities.

Explicit monotheistic statements come first from the prophet, Second Isaiah, of the late sixth century B.C.: "I am God, and there is no other" (Is. 46:9, etc.). Yet, there are many other passages prior to Second Isaiah which demonstrate Israel's exclusive commitment to Yahweh. Consequently, scholars have called the Mosaic faith practical monotheism or monolatry. At issue here is not a theory but a loving loyalty arising out of the personal relationship between Israel and Yahweh. Ancient Israel is not noted for its theoretical or philosophical propensity. Moreover, the biblical writings presuppose the existence of Yahweh from the outset and are not a textbook which attempts to prove the existence of God. They are rather a record of the people's living experience of God.

QUESTIONS FOR DISCUSSION

1. What are the facts which call for the source analysis of the Tetrateuch?

2. What are the major literary sources of the Tetrateuch?

3. In what sense should the biblical narratives be called "myths"?

4. How does the Priestly version of the "creation" account differ from that of the Yahwist?

5. In what way is God's creativity still operative in our world?

6. What is the meaning of "eating the forbidden fruit"? How do we ourselves also "eat" it in our own situation?

7. What did the exodus event mean to the ancient Israelites? How do we relate to this experience of liberation?

8. In what way can one practice the ancient biblical laws?

9. Trace briefly how the theme of human sin and God's saving activity is developed in Genesis.

10. What do you think you would do if you were in the place of a biblical person such as Adam, Eve, Cain, Noah, the patriarchs, or Moses? Choose one.

Chapter Two

THE DEUTERONOMIC WRITINGS

The literary bloc which includes the Book of Deuteronomy and the historical books (Joshua, Judges, 1 and 2 Samuel, and 1 and 2 Kings) is a product of the so-called Deuteronomist. The Deuteronomist is, according to scholars' consensus, an unknown theologian(s) who, inspired by the teaching of the Book of Deuteronomy, edited the Book and also wrote a series of historical narratives concerning Israel from the time of her settlement in Canaan (in the thirteenth century B.C.) to the fall of Jerusalem (in the sixth century B.C.). This historical work was completed shortly after the city's fall, and received an authoritative status in approximately 550 B.C. Consequently, it is appropriate for us to discuss Deuteronomy first and then proceed to these historical writings.

1. THE BOOK OF DEUTERONOMY

Original Book of Deuteronomy

This fifth book of the Old Testament has an intriguing origin. The nucleus of this book is an ancient "book of the law" discovered in the temple in Jerusalem in the eighteenth year of the reign of King Josiah (621 B.C.). Its historical background is this: the Israelites, after the sojourn in the wilderness, settled down in Canaan, and eventually established a kingdom (in the tenth century B.C.), which underwent historical ups and downs. Immediately prior to Josiah, the country experienced under King Manasseh (687–642 B.C.) a period which the Deuteronomist would call a dark age. This king enforced a pro-pagan policy in order to ingratiate himself with the mighty kingdom of Assyria by amalgamating the worship of Yahweh with that of Assyrian deities such as Baal and Ashrah. He built idols and altars for those gods and practiced magic and sorcery. Those who protested were put to death (2 Kgs. 21:16). Following Manasseh's death, his son, Amon, perpetuated the same policy as the king, but was assassinated after a two year reign. Upon Amon's death, his young son, Joshua, was placed on the throne, and, unlike his father and grandfather, became one of the most pious and capable rulers of Israel.

According to 2 Kings 22, the king, out of sincere religious devotion, ordered a rebuilding of the Jerusalem temple in the eighteenth year of his reign. In this constructive process, a law book was discovered and read before the king. The content of the book so greatly inspired him that he embarked upon a wholesale religious reformation of the country. Pagan idols, altars, and practices were annihilated, and the centrality of the temple for the genuine worship of Yahweh was established in Jerusalem. The king furthermore underscored the importance of the Passover festival, about which the Deuteronomic writer commented: "No such Passover had been kept since the days of the judges who judged Israel, or during all the days of the kings of Israel or of the kings of Judah" (2 Kgs. 23:22).

The provenance of this discovered law book is uncertain; some scholars conjecture that it was written by some prophetic group who fled to Jerusalem from the northern kingdom, Israel, as she fell to the Assyrians in 722 B.C. During the persecution by the apostate King Manasseh, the book was formulated with the intention of reforming worship and also of consolidating the whole people of God, both Israel and Judah.

The book was placed in the temple and then discovered in the time of Josiah.

The book's identification with the original form of the Book of Deuteronomy has been universally accepted because of the undismissible concurrences between Josiah's reform program and the religious tenets uniquely featured in Deuteronomy, viz., a cultic concentration (Deut. 12:11–14; 2 Kings 23:8, 9, 19) and a required pilgrimage to the central sanctuary for the Passover feast (Deut. 16:1–7; 2 Kings 23:21–23). This original part of Deuteronomy may well be identified with our Deuteronomy 12–36 which is a collection of law codes. Chapters 5–11 constitute the introduction to the main part, though they contain many additions and editorial alterations. The rest of Deuteronomy is, by and large, ascribed to subsequent editors.

Despite the fact that the whole book as we have it now appears as a farewell sermon delivered by Moses just prior to Israel's entry to Canaan, the promised land, Deuteronomy must be dated in the seventh century B.C. The reasons for this judgment are as follows: first, as we have observed, the law book discovered in the temple in 622 B.C. must be some form of the original Book of Deuteronomy. Second, Deuteronomy's laws have many parallels in Exodus 20:23–23:33 (the so-called Book of the Covenant), but Deuteronomy's version presupposes a later social background (compare, for example, Ex. 23:10ff. with Deut. 15:1ff.). Yet, Deuteronomy betrays no trace of the exilic and post-exilic legislation. Third, some distinctive influences of the eighth century prophet, Hosea, can be detected in Deuteronomy, and, moreover, Deuteronomy's literary style is similar to that of Jeremiah of the seventh century in many cases.

Deuteronomic Theology

From the foregoing observations regarding the background of Deuteronomy, the basic intention of its author is clearly understood: the reformation of a people lost in religious apostasy and political uncertainty. What then is the

Deuteronomic proposal for this reformation? To answer this question, Deuteronomy advances a distinctive theological thesis, which can be summarized by one word: oneness.[1] Oneness is applied, first of all, to one God; Yahweh is the unique God for Israel's exclusive devotion.

> Hear, O Israel: the Lord our God is one Lord; and you shall love the Lord your God with all your heart, and with all your soul, and with all your might (Dt. 6:4).

This strong admonition undoubtedly intends to call back from pagan deities the confused and straying Israel of the seventh century B.C. Yahweh is the only God who has bestowed upon them true loving care; he is the only God to whom they belong. Deuteronomy reiterates God's guidance through the exodus, the sojourn in the wilderness, and the settlement in the promised land ("rest" in Deuteronomy's term). God himself is the invisible, spiritual center of this nation. This is not simply abstract God-talk, but is a strong summons to the people to commit themselves in one covenant with one God. A firm personal relationship with God predicated upon the covenant would generate spontaneous devotion, trust, and obedience as a free response to God's love. Such a covenantal relationship between God and the people, as stressed in Deuteronomy, is not simply a matter of Moses' day but is valid also in the Deuteronomist's day.

Second, Israel is one integral nation whom God has chosen to carry out his will in history. The Israelites are a chosen people only because of God's love and not because of their superiority to other nations (Deut. 7:6–8). Therefore, they are required to observe God's ordinances with love. In this manner, Deuteronomy advances the theological ground for the nation's existence. The nation does not consist of some contingent gathering of people but of the persons whom God has called to come together to accomplish a divine mission in this world. Each member of this community is, therefore, expected to possess such a self-awareness. With this theological conviction, Deuteronomy intends to recreate the people of God as one coherent entity in the midst of political upheavals.

Third, there should be only one legitimate place for worship. As mentioned previously, this is one of the most distinctive assertions found in Deuteronomy. Nowhere else in the Old Testament do we encounter such a requirement. In fact, the older law insists upon just the reverse: "In every place where I [God] cause my name to be remembered, I will come to you and bless you" (Ex. 20:24). However, from the Deuteronomic perspective, it is a logical conclusion that one nation under one God should concentrate in one cult at one definite place. But this assertion is more than a theory; it not only completely purges pagan sanctuaries and practices but also puts forward the temple in the capital city as the tangible religious center by abolishing local sanctuaries of old Israel. This cultic concentration in Jerusalem thus contributes to the political and social unity of the nation.

Finally, there is one land—the land of Israel. This is the land which God promised to the patriarchs, and to which he led Israel through the wilderness from Egypt. Deuteronomy repeatedly underscores the goodness of this land as compared to that of Egypt and the wilderness. In no other place has God given his people the final "rest" (Deut. 3:20; Jos. 1:13–15, etc.). This land of rest is truly a tangible guarantee of the fulfillment of God's promise and assurance.

Such forceful centripetal theology of Deuteronomy has given spiritual impact to the ensuing periods of Israel and the later history of Jews and even Christians. The Jews of today, for example, still recite Deuteronomy 6:4 (quoted above) in a daily prayer. Deuteronomy is the most quoted Old Testament book in the New Testament (eighty-three times). Jesus says that the most important commandment is to love your God, which is taken again from Deuteronomy 6:4.

2. THE DEUTERONOMIC HISTORICAL NARRATIVE

The Deuteronomist's work is not history in the modern sense, but rather a theological commentary upon Israel's history. Despite a considerable diversity of material which stems from various older sources, it decidedly manifests a Deuteronomic theological propensity; historical incidents are judged from the point of view of obedience to the Deuteronomic command—above all else, exclusive devotion to God and to the cultic concentration in the central sanctuary.

The kings, for example, who violated any of these criteria, are condemned or neglected no matter how politically or militarily successful they might have been, while pious rulers are highly praised. Whether or not they are outstanding in a secular sense is not at all the writer's concern, because his conviction is that history is not just a sequence of human affairs but is a matter of God's concern as well. The world is an arena of interaction between God and people. Those who handle life only from their own perspective, no matter how skillfully or whatever their excuse, do not do justice to it or to God. Idol worship and divination practices are expressions of selfish desires which hinder people from seeing truth.

The Deuteronomist regards Israel's history more often than not as a series of apostasies that provoke divine judgment, the climax of which is the Babylonian exile. He hence does not hesitate to excoriate it and summon the people to return to the right way and to God. The call to repentance and return constitutes a central message of the Deuteronomist.[2]

The Entry and Settlement in Canaan

The Book of Joshua narrates Israel's entry and settlement in Canaan. These accounts picture the swift, organized, militaristic operations of the Israelite tribes led by Joshua. This picture, however, is an idealized simplification, since archaeological research has revealed no clear evidence of such an invasion and occupation during this particular period (from the end of the Late Bronze Age to the Early Iron Age). A generally accepted reconstruction depicts the Israelites' entry and settlement in Canaan as gradual.[3] The biblical record of their invasion from Transjordan into the central hill region seems to have historical basis, although there is no evidence that it had anything to do with Jericho and Ai. They appear to have stayed in these mountain territories until the monarchical period (in the tenth century B.C.) because of their incapacity for coping with the people of the lowlands, such as the Philistines who arrived by sea from the Aegean area at approximately the same time as Israel's arrival in Canaan.

The process of their tribal occupation in different territories was also slow and unorganized. Eventually the twelve tribes settled as follows: the tribes of Asher, Zebulun, Issachar, Naphtali, and Dan settled in the north (Galilee), Manasseh, Ephraim, and Benjamin in the central region, Gad and Reuben in Transjordan, Judah and Simeon in the South (Judah later absorbed Benjamin and Simeon). Most likely their intertribal association was rather loose at this stage, though the cohesion within each tribe was strong. The national consciousness of these tribes as one Israel did not really develop until King David established the monarchy (in the tenth century B.C.). Yet their faith in Yahweh was common and a basic conducive factor of their inner- and inter-tribal kinship and loyalty.

Judges

The period between the settlement and the establishment of the monarchy is called the period of judges. The Book of Judges contains the stories of these leaders of Israel's tribes. "Judge" is a term employed in English translation of the Old Testament for the Hebrew word *shofet*. It is not a good rendering since *shofet* does not mean a judge in our society. In ancient Israel, there were two kinds of "judges": one a military leader who, inspired by God, stood up to fight Israelite enemies (e.g., Gideon and Samson), the other a judicial and administrative official. In fact, the only military hero who also "judged" was Jephthah (Jgs. 11–12).

The period of judges was a time of cultural and social adjustment for Israel. It was a demanding situation, for they had to change their whole life-style from semi-nomadic to sedentary and from pastoral to agricultural. A long-term planning of earthly products became a priority which required agricultural knowledge and techniques, an economic scheme, and social sophistication.

It was for them a time of great temptation as well. The

Canaanites were more experienced in agriculture and had their own religion—often referred to as a fertility cult—which was closely related to the agrarian life. Their chief deity, known by the name of Baal (meaning "lord"), was believed to control the fertility of the land. Baal was a personification of the powers of nature. The aim of Baal worship was to gain divine favor—a proper amount of rain and sunshine, abundant crops, health, longevity, procreation, etc. Its religious rites were meant to induce this sacred potence; they usually took the form of a sexual orgy, sex itself being an act of fertility and procreation. By participating in those religious performances, individuals could integrate themselves into the beneficent rhythm of nature. Therefore, the world view of such a fertility cult was determined by natural cycle. World history consequently was to take a cyclical course; history would go nowhere except to repeat itself.

Israel's belief in Yahweh tendered a case of disparity against the Canaanites' worship of Baal. Though Yahweh was the God who would vitally concern himself with the well-being of people and nature, he was transcendent. (God is in us but not of us.) Here is a crucial difference between the biblical religion and ancient nature religions and even modern varieties of humanism. The biblical religion insists on a decisive discontinuity as well as continuity between God and the goodness of the world.

Another major difference between the religions of Yahweh and of Baal is found in their views of history. In fertility cults, there was no sense of direction or purpose. By contrast, there was a clear awareness of the purposefulness of history in Israel's faith; God gave promises to the patriarchs, led the Israelites out of the house of bondage, and finally gave them rest in the promised land. Throughout all these various stages of history, God "walked with them" (cf. 2 Sam. 7:6–7). Every moment of history was an unrepeatable step; no matter how trite and insignificant it might appear, each moment constituted an indispensable occasion in the whole context of history. Otherwise the world would not make sense!

Throughout Israel's history from the time of entry into Canaan, one of the persistent problems involved a series of confrontations and compromises with Canaanite religion and culture. The Deuteronomic theologian viewed Israel's history as a sequence of apostasy, yet he was also acutely aware of God's presence in the same historical realm. Such an understanding of history led him to narrate the period of judges according to a distinctive theological scheme: the rule of a judge—the people's apostasy—divine judgment (an enemy's attack)—their outcry and repentance—his salvation through a judge. The writer of the Book of Judges repeated this pattern like a rhythm. However, this repetition was not the same as the cyclical view of history, since the Deuteronomist perceived God's creativity turning the wheel of history toward the future. Thus the next scene of the historical drama unfolds—the monarchical period.

The Books of Samuel and Kings

The books of 1 and 2 Samuel and 1 and 2 Kings cover the monarchical period. The major topics in these writings run as follows: Samuel (1 Sam. 1–8), Saul (9–15), David (16–2 Sam.–1 Kgs. 2), Solomon (1 Kgs. 1–11), the divided monarchy (12–2 Kgs. 17), the Kingdom of Judah (18–25). As in the case of the Book of Judges and in the bulk of the historical literature of the Old Testament, the Deuteronomist extensively used in the Books of Samuel and Kings older sources which contained folklore, hero tales, tribal traditions, the lost "Books of the Chronicles of the Kings" (1 Kgs. 11:41; 14:19, 29, etc.), and a history of David's royal court (2 Sam. 9–20; 1 Kgs. 1–2). The last named source, in fact, has been recognized by scholars to be the oldest written history found in the Old Testament, i.e., it was written by a royal historian sometime slightly earlier than that of the Yahwist (tenth century B.C.). But the Deuteronomist's editorial hand is quite visible throughout these four books. Since we have considered already the Deuteronomist's theology, let us focus our attention now on some important historical aspects described in these books.

The Establishment of Israel's Monarchy

The Israelite tribes experienced a special crisis of Philistine oppression in the eleventh century B.C. This led them to adopt a monarchical system so as to cope with the threat of foreign pressure more effectively. The process of the establishment of the monarchy seems to have been an event of complexity. This fact is detected by the existence of conflicting views concerning the monarchy. One tradition preserved in 1 Samuel 9:15–10:8 tells us that Samuel, the last judge and one of the earliest prophets in Israel's history, took the initiative in selecting and anointing Saul as the first king of Israel, while, according to another tradition in 1 Samuel 8:1–22 and 10:17–27, Samuel yielded reluctantly to the people's demand for a king and anointed Saul after warning them that it would not please God. As against the former politically realistic view, the latter contention was prompted by a traditional theocratic ideal, i.e., God is the only true ruler.

Facing the powerful enemy, the ambivalent support of the people, and a serious lack of economic and military resources, Saul's career as the king involved a series of desperate struggles. His conflict with Samuel, who represented the old religious tradition of Israel, eventuated in Samuel's abandonment of him; this did particular damage to his political activity. His tragic life ended in battle against the Philistines at Mount Gilboa.

Samuel, having turned from Saul, anointed David of Bethlehem to be the next king. David proved himself to be perhaps the most capable king in Israel's history. He succeeded in defeating the Philistine army as well as warding off other threats from neighboring nations. Other big world powers of those days such as Egypt and Assyria were preoccupied with their own inner problems, which of course helped David greatly.

Furthermore, he skillfully united all of the tribes of Israel by establishing the new capital in Jerusalem, centrally situated between the north and south. The city was neutral not only because of its location, but also because it had been acquired from the Canaanites by his own troops—thus it was called "the city of David."

In addition to these military and political successes, his reign was marked by the religious achievement of bringing the Ark of the Covenant into the tabernacle in Jerusalem so as to secure the religious center of the country. The ark of the covenant was the container of the two tables of the Decalogue (1 Kgs. 8:21), which was believed to be an embodiment of God's presence (Num. 10:35–36). By placing the symbol of the traditional religious heritage in the new capital, the old tradition and the new reality were effectively joined, a feat which Saul failed to accomplish.

Solomon further developed the kingdom his father had left him by expanding foreign trade, particularly with Phoenicia and Egypt, and by undertaking extensive construction (e.g., the temple and palace in Jerusalem, which, according to 1 Kings 10:1–13, looked so splendid that when the Queen of Sheba saw it, "there was no more spirit in her"—she was dumbfounded).

The Davidic Zion Tradition

Thus the country now enjoyed political stability, social development, and economic prosperity. Under such conditions came cultural enlightenment. The Yahwist epic was compiled, and a new theological trend emerged, often called the Davidic Zion tradition.

This tradition stemmed from the conviction that God had bestowed a special blessing upon the house of David by entering into a covenantal relationship with David.

> I [God] will be his [David's] father, and he shall be my son. When he commits iniquity, I will chasten him with the rod of men, with the stripes of the sons of men; but I will not take my steadfast love from him, as I took it from Saul, whom I put away from before you [David]. And your house and your kingdom shall be made sure forever before me; your throne shall be established forever (2 Sam. 7:14–16).

This divine promise to David resulted in God's bestowing unconditional grace upon him. The unconditional nature of this covenant is also paramount in God's covenant with Abraham. Both of these covenants were of a promissory type, i.e., they were predicated solely upon God's oath. This covenantal type stood in contrast to the obligatory type of the Mosaic covenant, which required the people's pledge of loyalty as well as that of God. Another contrast can be observed in the fact that in both Abrahamic and Davidic covenants, their eternal validity was emphasized; even Israel's disloyalty would not revoke the covenant. They were, therefore, prompted by God's eternal steadfast love ("steadfast love" in 2 Sam. 7:15 is, in fact, synonymous with covenant).

In the Davidic covenant, kingship played a decisive role. That is, this covenant would guarantee the stability of society through the Davidic kingship. As the receiver of God's special favor and mission, David's function was vital in Israel's relationship with Yahweh. Here we may see an idealization of this king; in 2 Samuel 7:14, he was called God's son. The father-son imagery was used in covenantal context in the Old Testament (also in other ancient legal documents from the Near East). For example, we read in Psalm 2:7–8:

He [God] said to me [David],
"You are my son, today I have begotten you.
Ask of me, and I will make the nations your
    heritage,
and the ends of the earth your possession."

The idealization of David later generated the belief that God would send a Messiah (anointed one) from the house of David. This belief became one of the major trends in Jewish thought, and, still later, Christians identified Jesus, born in David's home town of Bethlehem, as the Davidic Messiah.

Yet, the dominant role played by the king should not undermine the sovereignty of God in Israel. This fact can be indubitably observed by comparing the Israelite kingship ideology with other dominant royal ideologies in the ancient

Near East such as Egypt, Mesopotamia, and Canaan. In Egypt kings were considered divine by birth, while in Mesopotamia and Canaan kings became divine at enthronement by being adopted by a god. In Israel's kingship ideology, no one (including kings) became a god: kings were to represent people before God and to carry out God's will. Kings were not allowed to exercise their ruling power by divine right. However, Israel's ideology was influenced particularly by their immediate neighbors, the Canaanites. We should recall the fact that Israel adopted the monarchical system in order that they might be "like all the nations" (1 Sam. 8:5). Some of the so-called royal psalms, which reflected the royal coronation ceremony, refer to the divine sonship of kings (e.g., Pss. 2:7; 89:27; cf. 2 Sam. 7:14), which nonetheless have no connotation of physical sonship, but indicate a special privilege bestowed by God.

Another significant factor of the Davidic Zion tradition is concerned with God's election of Jerusalem, i.e., God chose the temple of Jerusalem to be his sacramental dwelling place. We read in Psalm 132:13–14:

For the Lord has chosen Zion;
he has desired it for his habitation:
This is my resting place forever;
here I dwell, for I have desired it."

The idea expressed here is indeed momentous; until the birth of the Davidic Zion theology, God had never been believed to be permanently attached to any geographical locale. He had been said to have "walked with" Israel and her forebears. This drastic theological evolution was elicited by Israel's fresh awareness of God as the source of stability and also by the influence of the Canaanite idea of the temple as a house of God (the Jerusalem temple was designed by a Phoenician architect according to his native style). From this time on throughout the history of Israel and of later Jews, Jerusalem has been the center—a symbol of God's presence, of national unity and of hope.

The Divided Monarchy

After the death of Solomon, the unity of the nation collapsed, resulting in two kingdoms: the northern kingdom of Israel and the southern kingdom of Judah. Several factors may be cited as reasons. First, climatically and geographically, the northern part of Palestine differed from the south. The north was more fertile and closer to the economically and culturally more advanced territories like Phoenicia, Syria, and northern Mesopotamia, while the south was generally barren, less prone to foreign influence, and thus more conservative. Second, the kingdom was held together under David and Solomon mainly by their personal charisma and capability. When such personal leadership dissolved, the country was destined to experience a schism. Third, Solomon's extensive economic and industrial enterprises demanded heavy taxation and labor, causing widespread discontentment among the citizenry. Fourth, the Davidic Zion ideology antagonized the older theocratic traditionalists, particularly in the northern territory.

While the southern tribe of Judah remained loyal to Rehoboam, the son of Solomon, who succeeded to his father's throne in 922 B.C., the northern tribes under the leadership of Jeroboam (a former royal official and then a fugitive from Solomon's power) seceded from Jerusalem and established their own government in Shechem and, by erecting two golden calves at Dan and Bethel, their sanctuaries. (The calves were not really idols but were meant instead to be pedestals for the invisible Yahweh.) This course of action was a grave sin to our writer, the Deuteronomist, who stigmatized it as "the way of Jeroboam" (1 Kgs. 15:34; 16:2, 19, etc.).

In addition to tension caused by these two sister states, threats from outside were visited upon them as well—from the Egyptians and the Arameans. The former under Pharaoh Shishak, particularly, inflicted the country with extensive devastation (ca. 920 B.C.). Yet Israel gained stability as Omri (879–869 B.C.) assumed the throne and built a new capital at Samaria. During this stage of history, Israel and Judah were at peace. In Israel, Omri's son, Ahab, succeeded his father, following the same policy, and apparently was successful as is attested to by archaeological investigations at Samaria, Megiddo, and Hazor. His marriage with the Phoenician princess Jezebel, however, brought Baal worship to the country and caused vehement protest from pious Israelites such as the prophets Elijah and Elisha.

The Omri dynasty ended with a military coup led by the army general Jehu (842–815 B.C.), who, by annihilating every member of the Omri family and the Baal worshipers, established his own dynasty. During the first half of the eighth century B.C., both Israel and Judah experienced political expansion and economic affluence. Particularly under two contemporary kings, Jeroboam II (786–746 B.C.) of Israel and Uzziah (783–742 B.C.) of Judah, prosperity reached climactic heights.

After this period, both countries declined, notably because of the Assyrian threat. Out of desperation, Israel and Syria schemed to form an alliance of smaller states to prevent an Assyrian invasion. When Judah refused to join the coalition, the allied forces attacked Judah with the aim of forcing her to participate (the Syro-Ephraimite war in 733 B.C.). Judah responded by requesting aid from Assyria. This mighty kingdom swiftly advanced its troops and wiped out the feeble resistance of Syria and Israel. The existence of Israel thus inexorably came to an end; Samaria fell in 722 B.C.

Judah survived, but was destined to live under Assyrian pressure. King Hezekiah finally revolted with the support of Egypt. However, the revolt was suppressed by the Assyrian king, Sennacherib, who besieged Jerusalem. The city barely survived, but the king had to pay much tribute to the Assyrians. With the end of Hezekiah's revolt, the Assyrian power, culture, and religion began to have strong influence on Judah. As we have already mentioned in our discussion of the historical background of King Josiah's reformation, the genuine worship of Yahweh declined, and in its stead polytheistic religious practices flourished under Kings Manasseh (687–642 B.C.) and Amon (642–640 B.C.). Josiah (640–609 B.C.) was apparently successful not only in his religious attempts but also politically as he united the country. Assyria became weakened and was finally defeated by the Babylonians. This international vacuum aided Josiah considerably. However, when the Egyptians, wishing to keep an international balance of power, came up against the Babylonians, Josiah, who sided with Babylonia, was killed in battle at Megiddo (609 B.C.).

With the death of Josiah, the country disintegrated; it became a pawn of the power struggle between the strong kingdoms of Babylonia and Egypt. First it was subjected by Egypt, and then in 605 B.C. the Babylonian king Nebuchadnezzar routed the Egyptian troops at Carchemish, and Judah became a vassal state of Babylonia. However, following rebellion, Babylonian punitive action came swiftly and violently; Jerusalem fell in 597 B.C. King Jehoiachin, leading citizens and skilled craftsmen were deported to Babylonia (cf. 2 Kgs. 24). Nebuchadnezzar placed Jehoiachin's uncle, Zedekiah, on the throne in Jerusalem. He later revolted against Babylonia, which resulted in a thorough devastation of the country by the Babylonians; Jerusalem was leveled and a deportation was carried out a second time (586 B.C.).

Thus ended the monarchical period. The Deuteronomist reflected as follows: "For because of the anger of the Lord it came to the point in Jerusalem and Judah that he cast them out from his presence" (2 Kgs. 24:20). Our author, however, closed his historical work with a reference to the release from prison of the exiled king of Judah, Jehoiachin. He was allowed "a seat above the seats of the kings who were with him in Babylon" (2 Kgs. 25:28). With this reference, the author seemingly intended to end his writing with a hint of hope of future restoration.

QUESTIONS FOR DISCUSSION

1. What is the literary style of the Book of Deuteronomy?

2. In what sense, according to the Deuteronomist, is Israel a chosen nation? In what sense could Christians also be chosen by God?

3. What is the Deuteronomist's view of Jerusalem and the land of Israel? Are there basic differences between the opinions of Jews and Christians in this regard?

4. What kind of religion was the Canaanite fertility cult?

5. Comment on the statement of contemporary analyzers who have said that contemporary Americans are by and large not monotheists but worshipers of a modern "fertility cult."

6. Why has King David been considered an ideal king as, for instance, demonstrated by the use of the Star of David as the national flag of the modern state of Israel?

7. What kind of relationship emerged between religion and the kingship under David? How does this relate to the modern idea of separation of Church and state?

8. What was the significance of the temple? Is there any correlation between the meaning and function of the ancient temple and the modern Church?

Chapter Three

THE PROPHETIC TRADITION

1. WHAT IS PROPHECY?

There were three major strands within Israel's religious tradition: priestly, prophetic, and sapiential. Each of these three formed a distinctive body of teaching and a chain of Israel's heritage. Israelites attributed to them abiding trust and paramount authority as indicated in Jeremiah 18:18: "The law shall not perish from the priests, nor counsel from the wise, nor the word from the prophet" (see also Ez. 7:26). We will attempt in this chapter to elucidate "the word from the prophet," i.e., Israel's prophetic proclamation and activity as recorded in certain parts of the historical books and the prophetical literature of the Old Testament.

What is prophecy? It is a proclamation of God's message. Prophets are the ones who receive communication from God through inspiration and transmit it to the people. This type of religious activity appears to have taken place rather widely in the ancient Near East.[1] Biblical prophecy shared many common features with prophecies of that part of the ancient world. However, while a mystical divine-human fusion was usual in those prophetic movements, in Israel the awareness of Yahweh as distinct from humans was made extremely clear on the part of the prophets, i.e., no total absorption of the prophets' mind by the deity occurred even during an ecstatic state of inspiration. Consequently, Israel's prophets were not simply mouthpieces of God, but were also quite human as their own sensitivity and consciousness were indubitably at work. They were able to recognize problems of their world precisely and to perceive them in a divine perspective, and subsequently were able to crystallize their perception into language with intensity of feeling and insight.[2] The dynamism of this crystallization was so transparent and compelling that it caused the same effect as direct verbal communication with God. For instance, privy to God's heart, Amos declared: "Surely the Lord God does nothing without revealing his secret to his servants the prophets" (Am. 3:7).

They were men of courage as well; they possessed courage to speak up against authority and power, pointing out the problems, the solution, and the consequences. Thus their speeches about the future were not unrelated to the present; they were preaching concerning the here and now. These people were not fortune tellers with crystal balls.

2. THE DEVELOPMENT OF ISRAEL'S PROPHECY

The early prophetic movement in Israel is not clearly known,[3] but it is certain that there were some prophetic circles at the dawn of Israel's monarchy. Samuel was perhaps associated with "a band of prophets coming down from the high place (i.e., sanctuary)" (1 Sam. 10:5). This passage refers to prophets of those days who were highly ecstatic and also connected with local sanctuaries (the so-called cultic prophets).

After the monarchy was established, there were prophets who served in the royal court. Nathan, for example, transmitted a divine sanction to the Davidic dynasty (2 Sam. 7), but he also openly condemned David for his affair with Bathsheba (2 Sam. 12). In the court of Ahab, there were "four hundred prophets" (1 Kgs. 22:6). It was also under the reign of Ahab that the prophet Elijah confronted Baal's prophets and successfully demonstrated that Yahweh, not Baal, was to be worshiped as God (1 Kgs. 18). During the eighth century B.C.,

HISTORICAL CHART OF OLD TESTAMENT TIME

B.C. 1800

        The patriarchs (Gen. 12–50)

1400   Hebrews in Egypt

1300

        Exodus (Exod.–Deut.)

1200

        Settlement (Josh, Judg. 1)

1100   Judges (Judg., 1 Sam. 1–12)

        Samuel
1000   Monarchy (1 Sam. 13–1 Kings 11, 1 Ch. 10–2 Ch. 9)

900   Divided monarchies (1 Kings 12–2 Kings 17,
        2 Ch. 10–28)
         Elijah

800   Assyrian crises
        Fall of Samaria
         Amos, Hosea, Isaiah, Micah
700   Zechaniah, Nahum, Habakkuk, Obadiah

        Jeremiah

600

        Fall of Jerusalem and the exile
        Ezekiel
        Second Isaiah

500	Restoration
	Zerubbabel, Haggai, Zechariah
	Joel, Malachi
400	Ezra, Nehemiah
300	Greek domination
200	
	Maccabean revolt (1–2 Maccabees)
	The Hasmoneans
100	
	Roman domination

Israel's prophetic tradition marked a high point with the appearance of Amos, Hosea, and Isaiah. They were the earliest prophets for whom there are books in the Old Testament. These prophetical books were not written by the prophets themselves, but instead are the end products of the compilation and editing of the words and behavior of the prophets.

3. THE PROPHETS OF ISRAEL AND JUDAH

Amos

Amos was "a herdsman and a dresser of sycamore trees" (Am. 7:14) from Tekoa, a village south of Jerusalem, and was called by God to be a prophet. In the days of Amos (the middle of the eighth century B.C.), both Israel and Judah were experiencing an age of great prosperity under Jeroboam II in the north and Uzziah in the south. As Amos described, there were "those who lie upon beds of ivory . . . and eat lambs from the flock . . . sing songs to the sound of the harp . . . drink wine in bowls and anoint themselves with the finest oils. . . ." (6:4–6).

However, Amos saw hollowness in this affluence as numerous injustices were carried out behind the facade of prosperity. He could hardly suppress his urge to excoriate the

hypocritical reality—an urge he was convinced that God had
evoked within him. He thus violently deplored:

> They sell the righteous for silver,
> and the needy for a pair of shoes,
> they that trample the head of the poor
> into the dust of the earth,
> and turn aside the way of the afflicted;
> a man and his father go into the same maiden,
> so that my holy name is profaned;
> they lay themselves down beside every altar
> upon garments taken in pledge;
> and in the house of their God
> they drink the wine of those who have been fined
>   (2:6–9).

He uttered these words of condemnation in Bethel, a central sanctuary in Israel, although he apparently was addressing both Israel and Judah. The royal court and priests
countered him by issuing an order of expulsion (7:10–13).

Amos thus prophesied God's judgment by announcing the
coming of "the day of the Lord." Against the popular belief of
his day that the day of the Lord was to be a time of joyous salvation, Amos declared that it was to be the day of God's judgment—doomsday (5:18–20). This was truly prophetic irony.
Justice was not simply a social problem; it was of vital concern
to God. Without it, sacrificial rites, no matter how beautifully
performed, had no meaning whatsoever (5:21–24). Life without
sincere concern for others was equal to death.

> Seek good, and not evil, that you may live;
> and so the Lord, the God of hosts, will be with you,
> as you have said.
> Hate evil, and love good,
> and establish justice in the gate;
> it may be that the Lord, the God of hosts
> will be gracious to the remnant of Joseph
>   (Am. 5:14–15).

I [God] hate, I despise your feasts,
and I take no delight in your solemn assemblies.
Even though you offer me your burnt offerings ...
I will not accept them. ...
Take away from me the noise of your songs. ...
But let justice roll down like waters,
and righteousness like an ever-flowing stream
    (Am. 5:21–24).

The good life in the true sense should be the life which would seek justice for society.

Although invoking a series of harsh prophecies of judgment, Amos also promised that God would be gracious to "the remnant"—a small minority remaining—who would strive to live a truly human life (v. 15).[4] The prophecy of Amos was not a cold and stern teaching of morality, but it was truly an effusion of loving concern for the people, which was also an efficacious reflection of God's love itself.

Hosea

Hosea was a later contemporary of Amos. Little is known about his background, but most likely he was born, lived, and prophesied in the northern kingdom, Israel. The Israel of his day was rapidly declining and fell in 722 B.C. After the death of Jeroboam II (746 B.C.), the country was plunged into anarchy. Within the ten years following the king's death, Israel had five kings, three of whom seized the throne by force. In addition to such political and social turmoil, there was the widespread practice of Baal worship. The religious confusion must have been closely related to the social unrest of the day. More often than not, people tended to seek tangible idols in the midst of such unstable conditions.

In such a chaotic situation, the message of Hosea's prophecy was somewhat different from Amos' prophecy which revolved around the significance of social justice. Hosea found instead that the ills of his society resulted from the people's estrangement from God; thus his prophecy was more personal than social.

In the initial three chapters, we read a story about Hosea's own married life. He married a woman called Gomer who had participated in Baal worship (which, as we have previously observed, involved sexual orgiastic practices of the fertility cults).[5] She gave birth to three children out of perfidy. He once separated from her, but at God's word he returned to her. Some scholars have suggested that this story is to be taken as a fictitious allegory, but it shows no such imaginary character. Rather it intends to draw a living analogy of God's ineradicable love for his people. Through painful experience, Hosea learned and demonstrated to others the fact that God would continue his steadfast love for his disloyal bride, Israel.

Thus Hosea first addressed fierce criticism to the prevalent Baal worship among the Israelites: "Ephraim is joined to idols, let him alone. A band of drunkards, they give themselves to harlotry; they love shame more than their glory ... and they shall be ashamed because of their altars" (Hos. 4:17–19). Stop harloting with idols, commanded Hosea, and return to the true husband who has kept steadfast love. Return where you belong! In Hosea 6:6 we read:

For I [God] desire steadfast love and not sacrifice,
the knowledge of God, rather than burnt offerings.

The Hebrew word ḥesed, rendered here "steadfast love," is sometimes translated "covenantal love." It indicates the loyal love that binds persons together in covenant; the dynamism of steadfastness springs not merely from legal obligation but from an inner persistence that arises out of the love relationship itself. Another key word in this passage is "the knowledge of God." This knowledge is not a theoretical cognition, but a personal apprehension of reality through living experience. The Hebrew word for this knowledge sometimes implies a sexual union. Thus the knowledge of God involves a personal commitment to God and not merely the possession of a philosophical concept about God. Such loyalty and commitment in love between God and the people is, according to Hosea, what God desires.

However, despite the prophet's urging, Israel did not seek *ḥesed* and the knowledge of God, and she fell by the swords of the Assyrians.

Isaiah of Jerusalem

The Book of Isaiah is a composite literary entity. It can be divided into three sections (chapters 1–39, 40–55, and 56–66) because of the historical, literary, and theological differences. It is evident that the Assyrian crisis of the eighth century B.C. is the historical background of the first section, the nucleus of which should be ascribed to the prophet Isaiah who lived in Jerusalem at that time.

The second section, however, presents a different case: its historical background is toward the end of the exilic era (in the sixth century B.C.), for the rise of a new power, Cyrus the Great from Persia, is mentioned (44:28; 45:1). This section, moreover, consists entirely of poetry. The third section is best understood against the context of the post-exilic Jewish community. Consequently, the prophet of the first section is usually called Isaiah of Jerusalem (or First Isaiah), the second Second Isaiah, and the third Third Isaiah.

As suggested in 8:16, Isaiah's prophetic teachings were collected and preserved by his disciples. Modern scholarly inquiry has revealed that there are in chapters 1–39 numerous later expansions of and additions to the original words of the teacher by his followers. In fact, chapters 24–27 (eschatological prophecy), 34–35 (another group of eschatological prophecy), and 36–39 (historical narrative) are clearly detectable as later separate incorporations. Chapters 1–12 comprise mainly prophetic pronouncements concerning Israel and Judah, chapters 13–23 oracles against foreign nations such as Babylonia, Assyria, Philistia, and others, and chapters 28–33 oracles again concerning Israel and Judah.

First Isaiah apparently was born and lived in Jerusalem during the second half of the eighth century B.C. His background is unknown, but he seems to have belonged to the upper class citizenry of the capital city. Although nothing is suggested as to a close association with the religious establishment there, he began his prophetic career after a visionary experience of God at the temple of Jerusalem in the year of King Uzziah's death (742 B.C.). In Isaiah 6 where the prophetic call of Isaiah is described, four significant religious ideas are presented: (1) the holiness of God, (2) human self-awareness of impurity upon encountering the Holy One, (3) the holy purifying the impure, (4) God's sending the prophet with the message of judgment. God's holiness signifies the inscrutable mystery and otherness of God, which, upon encountering humans, invariably induces a sense of vile creatureliness in the human mind. Nevertheless, it does not simply indicate separation from human creatures, but it also demonstrates the dynamism of transforming impurity to purity, feebleness to strength. The experience of the holy God removed Isaiah's terror and inspired him to become a prophet. This experience of God gave a cornerstone to his prophetic activity.

At that time, his country Judah was facing a great crisis because of the Syro-Ephraimite war. "His [the king's] heart and the heart of his people shook as the trees of the forest before the wind" (Is. 7:2). Isaiah's prophetic counsel to them was:

If you will not believe,
surely you shall not be established (7:9).

Isaiah said that the assurance should come only from the holy God, not from some political maneuver or from indecisive perplexity. "Trust in the Lord"—this advice sprang from the conviction that none other than Yahweh, the Holy One, was the Lord of history. The first crisis passed when the Syria-Israel allied forces withdrew.

The second crisis was brought about by the Assyrians when they besieged Jerusalem after they had overrun Syria and Israel. Judah was shaken even more violently than before. Isaiah's conviction and teaching, however, never swayed. He repeated: "Trust in the Lord!"

Therefore thus says the Lord God,
"Behold, I am laying in Zion for a foundation a
    stone,
a precious cornerstone, of a sure foundation:
he who believes will not be in haste" (28:16).[6]

It was God himself who set the foundation for Jerusalem;
therefore it would never be destroyed! One who would believe
this fact should not be at a loss. Again Jerusalem was, in fact,
spared as the Assyrian troops returned home without overtak-
ing the city. Shortly after that, the Assyrian king Senacherib
was murdered by his own sons.

God's special blessing and protection of the chosen city
thus comprised a cornerstone of Isaiah's prophetic message.
Indeed, the Davidic Zion theology found its prophetic spokes-
man in Isaiah. Such a theological conviction should not be tak-
en as sheer optimism or superstitious reliance on the chosen
city. In fact, the force of his prophetic criticism of the people
in Jerusalem was as fierce as that of Amos and Hosea. Yet,
Zion was to him a special place where God would unfold his
intention. Many renegades would fall, he declared, but God
would leave in Zion a remnant who would be faithful to God
(Is. 37:32).

Also vital in Isaiah's prophecy is God's election of the
house of David:

Of the increase of his government and of peace
there will be no end, upon the throne of David,
and over his kingdom, to establish it,
and to uphold it with justice and with righteousness
from this time forth and for evermore.
The zeal of the Lord of hosts will do this (Is. 9:7).

Rulers of the Davidic lineage were to perform God's will
in order to bring about the ideal world of peace and justice.
Isaiah 9:2–7 and 11:1–9 provided subsequent generations with
a basis for a belief in a future ideal ruler, a Davidic Messiah.

Micah

The Book of Micah consists of three major parts: chapters 1–3 (judgment), 4–5 (salvation), and 6–7 (judgment). As many contemporary scholars contend, only the judgment oracles contained in the initial three chapters can safely be ascribed to Micah of the eighth century B.C., while the rest of the book seemingly was edited by an unknown person in the sixth century B.C.

The prophet Micah, a contemporary of Isaiah, was from the small rural town of Moresheth in Judah. No further information concerning his life is available except for the fact that, as he asserted, he had a mission: "But as for me, I am filled with power, with the Spirit of the Lord, and with justice and might, to declare to Jacob his transgression and to Israel his sin" (3:8).

It was the time of the Assyrian crisis, mentioned in the previous sub-section. Under such grave circumstances, he saw profound evil present in the capital cities of Jerusalem and Samaria. His rural background apparently prompted him to denounce fiercely the ills of urban life, but it also led him to sympathize with the downtrodden in the countryside.

Hear this, you heads of the house of Jacob
and rulers of the house of Israel,
who abhor justice and pervert all equity,
who build Zion with blood
and Jerusalem with wrong.
Its heads give judgment for a bribe,
its priests teach for hire,
its prophets divine for money;
yet they lean upon the Lord and say,
"Is not the Lord in the midst of us?
No evil shall come upon us."
Therefore because of you
Zion shall be plowed as a field;
Jerusalem shall become a heap of ruins,

and the mountain of the house a wooded height
    (3:9–12).

To his prophetic eyes, the apostasy and injustices that
arose from greed in these urban areas symbolized human sin
at its worst; this was a situation which could only incur God's
judgment.

In contrast to such harsh oracles of doom, we find as well
comforting prophecy of salvation recorded in the Book of Micah. Most scholars ascribe these hopeful proclamations to an
anonymous editor of the Babylonian exilic period (in the sixth
century B.C.). This editor attempted to inspire the exiled Jews
by prophesying their ultimate restoration. This scholarly
view, however, does not necessarily assume that every oracle
of salvation in this prophetical book, originated some two hundred years after Micah, has nothing to do with him at all. The
oracles of salvation are possibly based upon this eighth century prophet's genuine utterances.

Micah, like his contemporary Isaiah, most probably
prophesied a righteous "remnant" (4:6–7; 5:7–9), the ultimate
exaltation of Jerusalem (4:1–2), and the Davidic Messiah (5:2–
4). These passages, though likely touched by some editorial
hands, reflect the original prophetic messages of Micah. The
last of these quotations is particularly well known because it
is cited in the New Testament in reference to the birth of Jesus (Mt. 2:6).

But you, O Bethlehem Ephrathah,
who are little to be among the clans of Judah,
from you shall come forth for me
one who is to be ruler in Israel,
whose origin is from of old, from ancient days.
Therefore he shall give them up until the time
when she who is in travail has brought forth;
then the rest of his brethren shall return
to the people of Israel.
And he shall stand and feed his flock

in the strength of the Lord,
in the majesty of the name of the Lord his God.
And they shall dwell secure, for now he shall be
    great
to the ends of the earth (5:2–4).

Zephaniah

The Book of Zephaniah, which seems to preserve the genuine words of the prophet Zephaniah, includes (1) prophecies concerning the coming judgment against Judah (1:1–2:3; 3:1–7), (2) oracles against foreign nations (2:4–15), (3) the promise of salvation to the nations and Judah (3:9–13), and (4) the promise of restoration (3:14–20).

Little is known about the life of Zephaniah. The superscription of the book (1:1), which traces his ancestry back to King Hezekiah (715–687 B.C.), places him at the time of King Josiah (640–609 B.C.). From his vigorous criticism of cultic corruption, we may well consider him an active supporter of Josiah's reformation.

I will stretch out my hand against Judah,
and against all the inhabitants of Jerusalem;
and I will cut off from this place the remnant of
    Baal
and the name of the idolatrous priests;
those who bow down on the roofs to the host of the
    heavens;
those who bow down and swear to the Lord
and yet swear by Milcom;
those who have turned back from following the
    Lord,
who do not seek the Lord or inquire of him (1:4–6).

A distinctive theme of Zephaniah's prophecy is "the day of the Lord." We have already encountered this concept in Amos; it speaks of a time of divine judgment.

The great day of the Lord is near,
near and hastening fast;
the sound of the day of the Lord is bitter,
the mighty man cries aloud there.
A day of wrath is that day,
a day of distress and anguish, a day of ruin and
    devastation,
a day of darkness and gloom, a day of clouds and
    thick darkness,
a day of trumpet blast and battle cry
against the fortified cities and against the lofty
    battlements (1:14–16).

When the day comes, even Nineveh, the capital of Assyria and a symbol of power and arrogance, will be reduced to "a desolation, a dry waste like the desert" (2:13). This prediction was, in fact, accurate; Nineveh fell in 612 B.C. at the hand of the Babylonians, who later brought a catastrophic end to Jerusalem as well.

Zephaniah, nonetheless, also maintained a ray of hope in his prophecy. Like Isaiah and Micah, he talked about a righteous remnant:

For I will leave in the midst of you
a people humble and lowly.
They shall seek refuge in the name of the Lord
    (3:12).

Nahum

Nothing is known about the prophet Nahum except the short book containing only three chapters ascribed to him. This book, seemingly free from later editors' hands, comprises a series of excellent Hebrew poems describing God's judgment upon Nineveh. The great majority of these poetic passages appear to anticipate the imminent fall of the city, but others may very well have been added by the prophet after the catastrophic event (e.g., 1:15; 3:18–19).

The literary features of the prophecy have led some modern scholars to assume that it was recited as a part of the liturgy at the temple and dramatized the teaching of God's vengeance on the enemy.

Unlike the other prophets, Nahum never once refers to the subject of the sin of Israel. Instead he solely concerns himself with the bitter denunciation of Nineveh, the Assyrian capital which embodies cruelty, injustice, and ungodliness.

Woe to the bloody city,
all full of lies and booty—
no end to the plunder! (3:1).

It is Nahum's relentless conviction that God will never let evil thrive forever. No matter how much thwarted by rebellion, the prophet contends, history is ultimately under God's control.

The Lord is slow to anger and of great might,
and the Lord will by no means clear the guilty (1:3).

Nahum's God is the God of righteousness who never leaves the guilty unpunished. His wrath flames like a stormy fire, an expression of the intensity of his demand for justice. In face of such divine fury, even "the mountains quake ... the hills melt; the earth is laid waste ... the world and all that dwell therein" (1:5). With such a devastating power, God challenges evil like a mighty warrior: "Behold, I am against you. . . . I will burn your chariot in smoke, and the sword shall devour your young lions. . . ." (2:13).

The image of the divine-warrior found in the Old Testament (e.g., Ex. 15:1–18, etc.) stemmed from the Canaanite religious milieu. While the Canaanites used the image in their mythology of the gods' battle against chaotic forces, the Israelites applied it to Yahweh's acts against historical foes. It found a prophetic expression in Nahum's oracles against Nineveh.

Habakkuk

Like Nahum, the Book of Habakkuk contains only three chapters; these chapters are composed of (1) a dialogue between God and the prophet (1:1–2:5), (2) oracles of woe against an unspecified oppressive nation (2:6–20), and (3) a poetic prayer (chapter 3). Modern scholars often point out that Habakkuk, like Nahum, seems to have a cultic background; some have suggested the prophet wrote these chapters for actual use in liturgy at the Jerusalem temple.

The life of this prophet is obscure; however, what is known from his writings is his lament over the prevalence of violence and injustice in his world. The source of this malevolence of which he complains is not explicitly stated. Could the prophet have been referring to a callous and avaricious foreign nation like Assyria or Babylonia when he spoke of the "Chaldeans" who devastated other nations (1:6–11)? Or could he have been suggesting some domestic enemies of the prophet like Jehoiakim, the king of Judah (609–598 B.C.), and his followers (cf. Jer. 22:13–19)? Scholarly opinion varies as to the possible answers to these questions, but most authorities seem to place Habakkuk chronologically at the time of turmoil when Babylonia took over political dominance from Assyria.

Reflecting on the senseless happenings in his world, Habakkuk posed the question: "Why dost thou [God] make me see wrongs and look upon trouble?" (1:3). His answer was: "The righteous shall live by his faith" (2:4), i.e., the righteous person should live in this disturbing world with firm faith in God's eventual solution, God being the ultimate ruler of history. Later this passage was used by Paul as he elucidated the teaching of righteousness through faith (Rom. 1:17; Gal. 3:11).

Jeremiah

The Book of Jeremiah is one of the three large prophetical books in the Old Testament, the others being Isaiah and Ezekiel. Scholars have recognized in the material of this book three different literary forms: (1) the poetic oracles of Jeremiah are preserved in chapters 1–25, (2) the biographical narratives written by his close disciple, Baruch, sometime between 580 and 480 B.C., are recorded mostly in chapters 26–29 and 36–44, and (3) the material seemingly compiled by an unknown disciple of Jeremiah, who was also influenced by the Deuteronomic theology, is found scattered throughout the book and mixed with (1) and (2). All three groups are closely related; however, to these three main components of the book, many other oracles and historical narratives were further added by later editors.

Jeremiah was a prophet during the most critical time in the entire history of ancient Israel. He was born into a priestly family in Anathoth, north of Jerusalem. The beginning of his prophetic activity occurred around the time of the death of King Josiah in 609 B.C.[7] The tragedy began with the unfortuitous death of this pious king and ended in the destruction of the country by the Babylonians. Jeremiah acted as a prophet in Jerusalem even after the fall of the city until he was finally carried off to Egypt (and perhaps killed) by a rebel group.

As Jeremiah viewed it, all this tragedy was the result of the apostasy of the people. The perfidious condition of Judah, he declared, made her forfeit her special blessing of God, and therefore Isaiah's assuring prophecy of the inviolability of Jerusalem had been revoked. Like Hosea, Jeremiah used the analogy of marriage to describe the relationship between God and the people. The latter, however, had become a disloyal bride by prostituting herself to Baal and by neither keeping a firm belief in God nor practicing justice in her society. The consequence of all this sin was the Babylonian invasion. Jeremiah predicted imminent disaster by announcing the coming of the symbolic "enemy from the north" (Jer. 4). To Jeremiah, the Babylonians were God's chastising rod.

Despite Jeremiah's relentless pleas, counsel, and intercessory prayers which he believed to be his prophetic task, the people, including the political and religious leaders, were not willing to face reality and instead sought to rely on the existence of the temple, the supposed dwelling place of God. Standing in front of the main gate of the temple, Jeremiah

boldly preached against this belief by saying that the existence of the temple and the liturgy performed therein would
not guarantee the security of the city and the people who
lacked wholehearted devotion to God and genuine ethical concern. The people were making the temple a "den of robbers,"
declared the prophet (Jer. 7).

Because of such prophetic activities which were terribly
offensive to those who stubbornly indulged themselves in the
illusion of a false peace, Jeremiah had to submit to constant,
malevolent persecution. His life was endangered many times;
once, in fact, he was thrown into a waterless cistern where he
sank into the mire and was later fortunately rescued. His prophetic spirit, however, remained as strong as ever. As we read
in 20:9: "If I say, 'I will not mention him [God] or speak any
more in his name,' there is in my heart as it were a burning
fire shut up in my bones, and I am weary with holding it in,
and I cannot."

Doomsday came as Jeremiah had repeatedly warned. A
thorough destruction of the country and deportation of the
people took place. Jeremiah was allowed to stay in Jerusalem,
where he continued to act as a prophet. His prophetic concern
was now to give the people hope for the future. He prophesied
that God would establish a "new covenant" with his people,
which would not be like the old Mosaic covenant and the law
written on the stone tablets which they violated; the covenant
law would be written instead on their hearts.

> Behold, the days are coming, says the Lord, when I
> will make a new covenant with the house of Israel
> and the house of Judah, not like the covenant which
> I made with their fathers when I took them by the
> hand to bring them out of the land of Egypt, my cov-
> enant which they broke, though I was their husband,
> says the Lord. But this is the covenant which I will
> make with the house of Israel after those days, says
> the Lord: I will put my law within them, and I will
> write it upon their heart; and I will be their God, and
> they shall be my people (31:31–33).

The prophecy of the new covenant heralded a new beginning—a new phase of history and a new relationship with God which was sealed in the innermost recesses of the heart. Every external authority, including kings, priests, and the temple, was annihilated by the Babylonians, but the one real authority and inward source of life persisted which nothing could destroy, the inner presence of God. Despite the terrible experience of the country's destruction, Israel's religion found a new vitality in Jeremiah's prophecy of restoration through the new covenant.

Obadiah

This shortest book in the Old Testament is titled "The Vision of Obadiah." Nothing is known as to Obadiah's life, and the date of the book has been subject to debate. Some scholars are of the opinion that the book came from a cultic prophet of the sixth century B.C. The author intended to encourage the weary Jewish community of the early post-exilic period by using older prophecies of divine judgment against the enemy, Edom. However, many other critics favor the view that these prophetic words were delivered right after the fall of Jerusalem in 587 B.C.; during that period, the people of Edom exploited Judah's misfortune, which prompted Obadiah to denounce these people (Ob. 12; Ez. 25:12; Lam. 4:21). The Book of Obadiah thus appears to vividly reflect the country's anguish and bitter cries for justice during a national catastrophe.

The animosity between Israel and Edom can be traced back to the patriarchs' days (the friction between Jacob, the eponym of Israel and Esau, that of Edom; cf. Gen. 25:23; 27:39f.), and it continued on through the monarchical period. Obadiah predicted that Edom would be eventually humiliated and destroyed. The day of the Lord, a day of judgment for all nations, was near.

> For the day of the Lord is near upon all the nations.
> As you have done, it shall be done to you,
> your deeds shall return on your own head" (v. 15).

However, the Lord would spare some part of Israel. For the sake of this "remnant," the nation would be restored, "and the kingdom shall be the Lord's" (v. 21).

Ezekiel

The Book of Ezekiel, as we have it now, is the end result of a long and complex literary compilation of prophetic materials; some of them derive directly from the prophet and others from his disciples of his time and even of the post-exilic time. The book's content can be divided rather neatly as follows: (1) Ezekiel's prophetic call (chapters 1–3), (2) the oracles against Judah (chapters 4–24), (3) the oracles against foreign nations (chapters 25–32), and (4) the oracles of a future restoration of Israel (chapters 33–48).[8]

The prophet Ezekiel was a priest at the Jerusalem temple and was exiled to Babylon after the fall of the city. His prophecy included two major themes: judgment and restoration. Before the fall, he prophesied imminent destruction as God's judgment upon the people. He demonstrated it by using various, often very strange, symbolic words and behavior. Like other previous prophets, he also perceived the downfall of the country as a result of the people's sins which incurred God's wrath. In fact, according to his view, the entire history of Israel was a series of rebellions against God. However, this historical reality of the evil of the whole nation in no way lessened individual responsibility:

> The soul that sins shall die. The son shall not suffer for the iniquity of the father, nor the father suffer for the iniquity of the son; the righteousness of the righteous shall be upon himself, and the wickedness of the wicked shall be upon himself (Ez. 18:20).

The fall of Jerusalem in 587 B.C. marked a turning point in Ezekiel's prophecy. The theme now became the restoration of Israel, which unfolded again in a variety of symbolic presentations. In chapter 37, for example, we read about the vision of the valley of dry bones. The transformation of dry bones into "an exceedingly great host" certainly symbolized a restoration of the exiles to their homeland. The restoration was not simply to be a political re-establishment of the community but to be a new formation of God's people.

> A new heart I [God] will give you, and a new spirit I will put within you; and I will take out of your flesh the heart of stone and give you a heart of flesh. And I will put my spirit in you, and cause you to walk in my statutes and be careful to observe my ordinances" (Ez. 36:26–27).

This would be done so that "the nations will know that I am the Lord, says the Lord God, when through you [Israel] I vindicate my holiness before their eyes" (v. 23).

The vision of a new temple in the restored Israel (chapters 40–48) concludes the book. The section most likely came from an editorial hand during the post-exilic period, but its nucleus goes back to the prophet himself. It is a great vision of a new world comparable to the garden of Eden centered in a new city called "The Lord is there" (48:35).

Second Isaiah

Chapters 40–55 of the Book of Isaiah have been attributed to an anonymous prophet in exile, who is usually called Second Isaiah (or Deutero-Isaiah). He lived in Babylonia toward the end of the exilic period as is attested to by his explicit reference to Cyrus the Great, the king of the newly rising power, Persia (44:28; 45:1, 13).

His prophecy was an exultant message of salvation: the exiles would be set free to return to the homeland. His prophecy opened with a jubilant tone:

> Comfort, comfort my people, says your God.
> Speak tenderly to Jerusalem, and cry to her
> that her warfare is ended,
> that her iniquity is pardoned,

that she has received from the Lord's hand
double for all her sins.
A voice cries:
"In the wilderness prepare the way of the Lord,
make straight in the desert the way for your God"
(40:1–3).

The prophet portrayed this deliverance as the second exodus—God himself would lead his people through the wilderness to the promised land. This new exodus would not simply be a political event; it also would be a disclosure of God's glory to all mankind:

Behold, I [God] am doing a new thing;
now it springs forth, do you not perceive it?
I will make a way in the wilderness
and rivers in the desert (43:19).

There are several distinctive theological assertions made by Second Isaiah. First, he conceived this deliverance in an eschatological perspective—the end of the whole historical drama and the beginning of a new era of God. Consequently, this "end" is a new beginning, a new creation. In fact, "to create" and "to redeem" were words used synonymously by the prophet.

Second, this event would provide the occasion to let the world recognize that Yahweh is the only God. "I am the first and I am the last; besides me there is no god" (44:6). This is the first and most explicit statement of monotheistic faith in Israel's history. To be sure, this monotheistic statement was made not in a theoretical context but strictly in a context of religious experience, i.e., within the context of the experience of salvation. The people should seek the one and only God, for he would give them ultimate freedom and would transform chaos (meaninglessness) to cosmos (meaningfulness). He was the only ultimate source of meaning in human life.

The third distinctive theological assertion of Second Isaiah involves the "suffering servant of Yahweh." There are four poems which specifically describe this enigmatic figure (42:1–9; 49:1–6; 50:4–9; 52:13–53:12). In the first poem, he is said to have been chosen by God, possessing a divine spirit, and bringing forth justice to the nations. The second poem tells how he will gather Israel and bring her back to Yahweh, who will cause her to be a light to the nations, spreading God's salvation to the ends of the earth. The third poem is an autobiographical speech by the servant; though oppositions and persecutions beset Israel, he continues to be faithful to God and divine instruction. The fourth poem portrays him as one who suffers terribly even to the point of death but whose suffering has a vicarious meaning:

> Surely he has borne our griefs and carried our
>   sorrows;
> yet we esteemed him stricken, smitten by God, and
>   afflicted.
> But he was wounded for our transgressions,
> he was bruised for our iniquities;
> upon him was the chastisement that made us whole,
> and with his stripes we are healed (53:4–5).

Therefore, God glorifies him.

Who then is this servant? Many differing views and scholarly theories have been presented, yet none of them is conclusive. The servant has often been interpreted to be the idealized Israel and, in fact, he is called Israel in 49:3. The New Testament writers and subsequent Christians traditionally applied the figure to Jesus (Mt. 8:17; Mk. 9:12; Lk. 22:37; Jn. 12:38; Acts 8:26–39, etc.). Or could it be the prophet himself? A mythological figure? Or some historical individual such as Moses, Jeremiah, Josiah, etc.? The ambiguity of information pertinent to the question in these four poems, as well as in the entire prophecy of Second Isaish, prevents us from reaching a fully convincing answer. At any rate, we have here the sparkling peak of Hebrew prophetic inspiration—above all, the un-

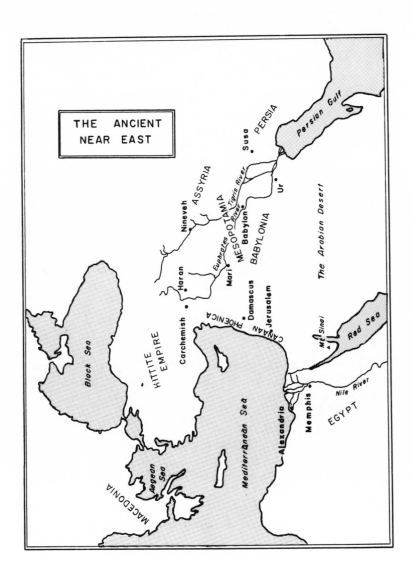

THE ANCIENT
NEAR EAST

PERSIA

Persian Gulf

Susa

ASSYRIA

Tigris River

Nineveh

MESOPOTAMIA

Euphrates River

Babylon

Ur

BABYLONIA

The Arabian Desert

Mari

Haran

Damascus

Carchemish

PHOENICIA

Jerusalem

Mt. Sinai

Red Sea

HITTITE
EMPIRE

CANAAN

Black Sea

Memphis

Nile River

Mediterranean Sea

Alexandria

EGYPT

Aegean
Sea

MACEDONIA

73

derstanding of vicarious suffering which brings about victory through suffering.

QUESTIONS FOR DISCUSSION

1. What kind of people were the Hebrew prophets? Are there modern prophets?

2. What did the prophets say about questions pertinent to human rights? What kind of significance do their teachings have in our own society?

3. What did the prophets say about the judgment of God? In what way can we talk about divine judgment in a modern context?

4. What is Hosea's concept of *ḥesed?* What would be its ramification in our life situation?

5. What idea of holiness is expressed in Isaiah 6? How does it differ from the modern concept of holiness?

6. Why did Jeremiah violently criticize the people's reliance on the temple (cf. Jer. 7)? What relevance is there of such criticism for present-day Christians' attitudes toward the Church?

7. Explain the concept, according to Jeremiah and Ezekiel, of "individual responsibility for sin." Compared to this concept, what kind of awareness of sin do modern people have?

8. Read the servant songs in Second Isaiah's prophecy carefully and discuss who the servant of the Lord possibly is.

Chapter Four

DEVELOPMENT IN THE
POST-EXILIC PERIOD

1. THE RESTORATION

As Second Isaiah had expected, the Persian king, Cyrus, conquered Babylonia and issued the decree that allowed the Jewish exiles to return to their homeland (538 B.C.). This event produced various effects of great significance. First of all, political dominance in the ancient Near East shifted from the hand of the Semites to that of the Aryans. Secondly, this new Aryan culture and religion thenceforth became predominant in the Western hemisphere. The religious tradition of Israel was thus influenced in many respects.

The returned Jews, led by Zerubbabel, who became a governor of Judea, and the priest Joshua, succeeded in restoring the altar in Jerusalem (cf. Ezr. 3). Their attempts at rebuilding the temple, however, were considerably hampered by trouble which developed with their neighbors. These neighbors were mixed groups of remnants of the old Israel and those who were transplanted from outside by the conquerors. Upon the Judaeans' refusal to accept the cooperation of these racially mixed people in the temple construction, the latter reacted by disrupting the work, which was, in fact, halted until the second year of Darius I (520 B.C.). The prophets Haggai and Zechariah urged Zerubbabel, Joshua, and the Judaeans to renew the building effort by proclaiming the arrival of a messianic age. Although personal details pertinent to these two prophets are confined only to the role they played in the incipient stage of rebuilding of the temple, there are two small books with their names attached.

2. THE PROPHETS AND LEADERS OF THE POST-EXILIC PERIOD

Haggai

The Book of Haggai comprises four discourses, each of which is dated from the sixth month to the ninth month of the second year of King Darius (520 B.C.) His prophetic words center around a single theme: the reconstruction of the temple. It was his firm conviction that the restoration of God's people should begin with the rebuilding of the house of the Lord. As long as it was left as a heap of ruins, he declared, the promised messianic age would never arrive. The splendor of the renewed temple was to be "greater than the former" (2:9). To Haggai's mind, this was to be a decisive moment in history; it would usher in the long-awaited messianic time when God would appear in his glory (1:8). Haggai considered Zerubbabel to be the Davidic Messiah whom God had chosen. The people who returned from the exile were the "remnant" of whom many of the prophets had prophesied.

Thus the prophet urged, "Now take courage, O Zerubbabel, says the Lord; take courage, O Joshua, son of Jehozadok, the high priest; take courage, all you people of the land, says the Lord; work, for I am with you" (2:4). As reported in 1:14, "the Lord stirred the spirit" of these people, who "came and worked on the house of the Lord of hosts, their God." Responding to their effort, Haggai told them: "From this day [the day of laying the foundation of the temple] on I [God] will bless you" (2:19).

Zechariah

The present Book of Zechariah is a composite product—a feature which reminds us of the Book of Isaiah. Only the initial eight chapters concern the prophet Zechariah, a contemporary of Haggai, while the remaining chapters (9–14) consist of several different units of prophecy. Many of these units seem to have come from later periods, for (1) there is no reference to the rebuilding of the temple, (2) the Greeks are mentioned in 9:13, and (3) the apocalyptic tone is dominant, a particular quality which embraces visions of the future victorious splendor of Judah.

Zechariah's prophecy recorded in chapters 1–8 can be divided into three main parts, each introduced by date headings which encompass the period from 520 to 518 B.C.: (1) the call to repentance (1:1–6), (2) eight visions (1:7–6:15), and (3) oracles concerning fasting and the messianic era (chaps. 7–8).

The central concern of Zechariah was to continue encouraging the work of restoring the temple, although the scope of his prophecy is wider than Haggai's. We find that it is around this theme that the series of Zechariah's visions revolve: God's re-election of Jerusalem, his appointment of Zerubbabel and Joshua as political and religious leaders, and his punishment of the wicked in the world. The visionary prophecy of Zechariah, alongside that of Ezekiel, certainly paved the way for the Jewish apocalypticism which blossomed particularly during the last two centuries B.C.

Zerubbabel, whom Haggai and Zechariah deemed a messiah, appears to have met an ill-fated end; we hear nothing about him thenceforth. Perhaps he was deposed by the Persians or assassinated. Despite the enthusiastic words of prophetic encouragement, the Jews had to continue struggling in the turbulent world. The fulfillment of divine promise was yet to come.

Joel

Because of a lack of evidence, it is extremely difficult to date the Book of Joel; scholars, in fact, vary in their views, as-

signing the book to a time anywhere between the pre-exilic
and the post-exilic periods. But the post-exilic date of origin
seems more plausible, for the historical background of Joel's
prophecy is more reasonably found sometime prior to the powerful emergence of Alexander the Great of Macedonia in 336
B.C.

Except for the prophetic sayings recorded in this book,
nothing else is known about Joel. His prophecy was apparently occasioned by a terrible locust plague, as he vividly described its disastrous effect. For the prophet, this misfortune
suggested something much more important than a mere natural calamity, i.e., it was a sign of divine judgment, the day of
the Lord. He described it by using an apocalyptic image: "The
earth quakes before them, the heavens tremble. The sun and
the moon are darkened, and the stars withdrew their shining"
(2:10). The prophet went on to call the people to repentance.
If they would wholeheartedly return to God, he said, God
would grant them fertility and prosperity.

> Return to the Lord, your God,
> for he is gracious and merciful,
> slow to anger and abounding in steadfast love,
> and repents of evil" (2:13).

Malachi

This last of the Old Testament prophetical books most
likely constituted the third section of a collection of prophecies, the first being Zechariah 9–11 and the second Zechariah
12–14. These three sections were each titled in a similar way:
"An oracle of the word of the Lord." While the first two were
somehow added to the Book of Zechariah, the third section
was left as an independent book. In fact, "Malachi" might
very well not have been a personal name; most likely it was
something of a byname chosen by an editor on the basis of the
Hebrew word for "my messenger (*mal'akhi*)" in 3:1. For convenience, we call the author of this book Malachi.

Malachi's prophecy comprises six oracles: (1) God's special
love for Israel (1:2–5), (2) a condemnation of the priests for

their failure to provide the people with a moral and spiritual ministry (1:6–2:9), (3) a denunciation of mixed marriages and divorce (2:10–16), (4) God's demand for justice and his judgment of the wicked (2:17–3:5), (5) a criticism of the people's failure to offer tithes (3:6–12), and (6) God's favoring of the pious (3:13–4:3).

These items which the prophet dealt with included the common practical problems that existed in the Jewish community of the post-exilic period. As we will observe in the next section, the question of marriage with foreigners was one of the controversial issues of those days. In general, after the reconstruction of the temple (515 B.C.), a mood of apathy prevailed among the people as the political and economic condition showed no sign of improvement and the promised golden age was not yet in sight. They asked, for example, "Does God truly care for us with love and justice?" "What is the good of our keeping his charge?" Consequently, the people tended to be lax morally and religiously. It was the prophet's task to bring them back to God and to stir up in them moral awareness.

It was not only Malachi who struggled with all those problems; there were others who shared in the effort. Among them there were such eminent figures as Ezra and Nehemiah, of whom we will make mention in the next section.

Ezra and Nehemiah

As referred to previously, Jewish history during the time between the reconstruction of the temple and the arrival of the Greeks in the late fourth century B.C. is an extremely beclouded period because of a lack of historical data. According to the Books of Ezra and Nehemiah, this period was the time when Ezra and Nehemiah generated social and religious reform among the Jews.

A vexing question here is the chronology of their activities; although in the biblical narratives Nehemiah appeared on the scene about twelve years later than Ezra, there are some ambiguities in the biblical information. Hence, scholars insist that the biblical material has reversed their chronological order; yet the historical emendation has not solved the question. In fact, there are some prominent scholars today who still hold to the basic accuracy of the biblical arrangement,[1] which we follow for our present purpose.

Ezra, "a scribe skilled in the law of Moses" (Ezr. 7:6), returned from Babylon in 458 B.C. with a lawbook, which he read to the people. It is beyond our ability to determine whether it was the entire Torah or only a part of it (e.g., a portion which we now call the Priestly source). The public reading of the Mosaic law ended with a ceremony in which the people confirmed their commitment to the law and renewed the ancient covenant (Neh. 8–10). Ezra vigorously enforced a policy against mixed marriage; he not only forbade marriage with non-Jews but also demanded divorce of men who had foreign spouses. This was an attempt to preserve Jewish national identity against overwhelming foreign pressure and influence.

Nehemiah, who had been serving at the Persian royal court, came to Jerusalem in 455 B.C., having heard of the rueful state of the city. Despite various difficulties, he successfully inspired the people to build the city wall. He then reformed the temple—in particular, the way in which the temple personnel raised revenue. Like Ezra, he also took vigorous measures against mixed marriages.

Thus under the leadership of Ezra and Nehemiah, the returned Jews established a theocratic community based on the law. This fact led later people to call Ezra, the promulgator of the law, the father of Judaism.

3. GREEK DOMINATION

During the middle of the fourth century B.C. the first Aryan world power, the Persians, were overpowered by a new force from the West. The young Greek king Alexander the Great decisively defeated the Persian troops at Issus in 333 B.C., extended his power as far as the Indus Valley, and thus established the Greek empire. He was an ardent believer in the Hellenistic culture and attempted to transplant it in any conquered lands. Consequently, Greek towns were built in various places (e.g., Alexandria in Egypt), and the Greek language began to be used as a universal tongue. The Jews, therefore, lived under Greek dominance for more than two hundred years. In fact, many Jews lived in Greek towns outside their homeland; and in Alexandria there was a sizable Jewish population which necessitated a Greek translation of the Hebrew Scripture (the Septuagint).

After Alexander's death in 323 B.C., Palestine was controlled by one of his generals, Ptolemy, who established a dynasty in Egypt. Under Ptolemy's rule during the third century B.C., the Jews enjoyed a relatively peaceful time. But in the ensuing century when another Greek power from Syria, the house of Seleucus, gained dominance in Palestine, the Jews encountered a fearful oppressor in Antiochus IV (175–163 B.C.).

Antiochus IV vigorously imposed a heavy tax as well as the Hellenistic culture and habits on the Jews, who responded in diversified ways. A pro-Greek faction was led by the Tobiad family and Jason (a brother of the then high priest, Onias III). They sent a bribe to the king and also made efforts to Hellenize Jerusalem through the construction of Greek-style buildings and other measures. As a result of those desperate struggles, Onias was killed, and Jason himself was outbid for office by Menelaus who was not from the priestly family. This series of ugly conflicts among the Jewish leaders accelerated the tyranny of Antiochus. He ordered the Jews to offer sacrifices to pagan idols, even in the Jerusalem temple. He forbade them to practice the ancestral laws, including circumcision and the sabbath, and he mercilessly slaughtered those who opposed him.

4. FROM THE MACCABEAN REVOLT TO HEROD THE GREAT

An increasing anti-Greek feeling among the Jews finally exploded under the leadership of the pious priest Mattathias and his sons. They were joined by the Hasidim (pious ones) who sought religious freedom, though without political ambition. Judas, the third son of Mattathias, who took leadership after his father's death, fought bravely against the Greeks. He was nicknamed Maccabee ("hammer" in Greek), which became the name of the revolutionary movement as a whole. The revolt was successful; Judas and his army recovered Jerusalem and rededicated the temple in 164 B.C. The Jewish festival of Hanukkah commemorates this event.

The victory produced religious freedom for the Jews. The Hasidim consequently withdrew from the battle with the Greeks. The Maccabeans, on the other hand, continued their struggle to establish complete political freedom as well, only to fall during battle. However, Simon, the second son of Mattathias, succeeded in gaining concessions from the Greeks and became a political and religious leader of the Jews. Under Simon (141–135 B.C.), the Jews won a degree of independence not only from the Greeks but also from the Romans, who became the dominant world power by defeating the Greeks in the first century B.C. From then on until the Roman conquest of Jerusalem in 63 B.C., Simon and his family (called the Hasmoneans) assumed, as priest-kings, rule over the Jews.

The Hasmonean dynasty ended in an ugly and bloody feud within the family. It was the family of Herod from Idumea (a non-Jewish province in southern Palestine) that arose to power by taking advantage of the chaotic situation in Judaea and procuring favor from Rome. In 37 B.C., Herod the Great was appointed king over Judaea, Samaria, Galilee, and Peraea.

Herod was shrewd in his maneuvers with the powerful in Rome, ruthless against his opponents, and excellent as a warrior. In fact, as a vassal of Rome, he was more Roman than Jewish; he paid no respect to Jewish law and made every attempt to establish the Roman temple, amphitheaters, baths, palaces, etc. His thirst for grandeur drove him to inaugurate a thorough rebuilding of the temple and palace in Jerusalem. The age of Herod's reign (37–4 B.C.) was, in spite of his utter unpopularity among the pious and nationalistic Jews, relatively peaceful.

5. SOCIO-RELIGIOUS INSTITUTIONS AND SECTS

From the time of the Deuteronomic reformation, the temple in Jerusalem was the only center of Jewish life and religion. Pilgrimages to the temple for the annual festivals (Passover, Pentecost, and Tabernacles) were required. In the temple the high priest with the help of many other lower-ranking priests officiated at sacrificial ceremonies. Closely connected with the temple was the Sanhedrin (from Greek *synedrion* meaning "council"), which, presided over by the high priest, handled legislative and judicial matters. Synagogues (from Greek *synagoge*, "assembly") were located not only throughout Palestine but also in numerous Jewish towns outside of Palestine. Each synagogue was a house of prayer and a center for religious education conducted by rabbis (from Hebrew *rab*, "master," i.e., teacher). After the Roman destruction of Jerusalem in A.D. 70, only the synagogue and rabbinical leadership—and not the temple, priesthood or cult—survived.

There were three major sects of Judaism at least during the last two centuries B.C. and the first century A.D.: the Sadducees, the Pharisees, and the Essenes. The origin of the Sadducees is uncertain; it has been held that the name came from Zadok, the high priest under Solomon (1 Kgs. 2:35). This sect consisted chiefly of priests and lay aristocrats. The Jewish historian, Josephus, of the first century A.D., noted that they were an active party during the second century B.C. They must have played a dominant role at the temple and in the Sanhedrin. Again for lack of information, little is known about their teachings, though they apparently rejected the oral law and such doctrines as belief in the resurrection and in angelic and demonic spirits. They accepted only the written law (Torah) which included none of these ideas. The destruction of the temple (A.D. 70) seems to mark the end of their existence.

"Pharisee" presumably came from the Hebrew word, *parash,* meaning "to separate." It is not clear, however, what it implies (a separation from uncleanliness, or from the negligent masses called *Am Haarez,* or from the Maccabeans). The word can also mean "to interpret," i.e., interpretation of the law. The Pharisees were an offshoot of the Hasidim. As descendants of those pious ones, they were perfectionists in observing the law, which included the oral law so as to make the Mosaic law more applicable to changing conditions. Hence they were more progressive than the Sadducees and advocated such teachings as resurrection, future punishment and rewards, angels and demons, and the Davidic Messiah. This group consisted mainly of lay people of the middle class and was more hostile toward foreign oppressors than the Sadducees. After the city's destruction, only this sect survived, and it re-established Judaism even without the temple and the homeland (rabbinic Judaism).

The third major Jewish sect was the Essenes. Since the discovery (dating back to 1947) of the Dead Sea Scrolls, it has been widely recognized that the Essenes were a group of Jews who established a monastic community at Qumran on the northwest shore of the Dead Sea in the second century B.C. and who left these scrolls and fragments in nearby caves as the Romans destroyed their community in A.D. 68. From the information given by these documents, the site and other sources (e.g., Josephus and Philo), scholars have reconstructed their history and determined that they, like the Pharisees, were an offshoot of the Hasidim, separating themselves from the surrounding unlawful society in order to live communally and to devote themselves to study and strict observance of the law. They also ardently entertained an apocalyptic belief in the eschatological kingdom of God.

In addition to these three major sects, there was another highly militant group called the Zealots, who, out of religious and nationalistic zeal, did not hesitate to take up the sword against the Romans. There were also many other smaller groups, little of which is now known.

6. HOPE FOR THE FUTURE

To Israel, world history was not a repetitive, cyclical movement comprised of meaningless events like that pictured in the Greek myth of Sisyphus whose fate it was to push a rock up a hill only to have it always roll down again as soon as he had brought it to the summit. By contrast, to Israel, history was a process of interaction between God and the people with a definite beginning and ending. Therefore, no matter how absurd individual events might sometimes appear, there was meaning and purpose to life. Always there was the hope that God would meet people in the future as he had in the past. This belief in God and hope for the future provided fertile soil in which Israel's messianism, eschatology, and apocalypticism could be born and nurtured.

In time of crisis, consequently, Israelites sought the favor of God, asking him to send them a mighty and pious ruler, the Messiah (the Anointed One). As we have observed in the previous chapter, Isaiah of Jerusalem (9:6–7; 11:1–5), Micah (5:2–4), Jeremiah (23:5–6), and Ezekiel (34:23–24; 37:22, 24–25) referred to an ideal king who would come from the house of David. Haggai and Zechariah expected Zerubbabel to be a messianic figure for restoration of the nation. Such a messianic hope gained momentum naturally during the turbulent years from the Hasmonean period down to the New Testament period.

People expected that the Messiah, sent from God, would crush the oppressors and the wicked, so as to establish a world of God, where justice and peace would prevail. This belief is attested to by some of the Jewish writings of these periods (certain portions from the Apocrypha, the Pseudoepigrapha, and rabbinic writings, such as 1 Enoch, 2 Esdras, 2 Baruch, the Psalms of Solomon, and others). The Dead Sea Scrolls also reveal a deep strain of messianism. The New Testament finds in Jesus of Nazareth the long-awaited Davidic Messiah.

Another component of great significance in the Jewish hope for the future is eschatology (from Greek *eschatos* meaning "last"). Eschatology involves teachings concerning the end (or a drastic transformation) of this world. As we have mentioned above, the ancient Jews firmly believed that God was the ultimate director of history—a history that would reach its culmination through God's judgment of the wicked and the saving of the righteous. It would be a time of recreating the universe. World history constituted one purposeful unity. Since the days of the prophet Amos, who preached the coming of the day of the Lord, such a belief in the final arrival of God was underscored particularly by the prophets. It became a prominent theme during the exilic and post-exilic periods as represented by Ezekiel 36–48, Second Isaiah, and many others.

During the late post-exilic period, the prophetic eschatology found its offshoot, i.e., apocalypticism (from Greek *apokalyptein*, meaning "to reveal"). Scholars once sought the provenance of this Jewish religious trend in the Persian religion, Zoroastrianism, but the most recent scholarly consensus tends to draw a closer line of development between prophetic eschatology (Second and Third Isaiah and Zechariah 9–14, in particular) and apocalypticism. However, this development was not a simple and direct process but was highly complex owing to various influences ranging from old mythological images and motifs to the wisdom tradition (cf. next chapter) in Israel as well as influences from the outside, e.g., Persia and the Hellenistic world. At any rate, as a continuation of prophetic eschatology, apocalypticism was basically concerned with history as the arena of God's judging and saving acts and, above all, with the apex of this historical process—the end.

However, apocalypticism was different from prophetic eschatology in the sense that the former had a characteristically other-wordly orientation. This basic nature was prompted by the despondent political and social conditions of the times. Apocalyptists (who characteristically remained anonymous)

belonged to an oppressed group who cried out to God for justice. They consequently envisaged sharply opposing worlds—
the good and the evil. The present world was an era dominated
by the children of darkness, who would be destroyed by God,
thereby ushering in a new world of peace and justice. Apocalyptists pictured this process in a highly symbolic and visionary fashion by featuring a final cosmic war between good
(angelic) and evil (demonic) forces. They claimed that everything in history had been precisely determined by God, and
that God had revealed secret mysteries concerning when and
how the whole drama was to be historically enacted. This historical determinism was another distinctive feature of apocalypticism.

The first half of the Book of Daniel, 1 Enoch, and 2 Esdras are some representatives of
Jewish apocalyptic literature. Only the first of these is includ-
ed within the Old Testament canon. The Book of Daniel is
unique among the Old Testament because of its apocalyptic
nature. It was written by an anonymous author, most likely
one of the Hasidim, during the persecution by Antiochus IV.

The first half of the Book of Daniel (chapters 1–6) portrays
Jewish pages of the Babylonian royal court—Daniel (the name
taken from an ancient legendary righteous man; cf. Ez. 14:14;
28:3) and his friends. They were pious ones who were loyal to
the ancestral law even to the point of risking their lives (chapters 1, 3, 6). The narratives concerning the Babylonian king,
Nebuchadnezzar's insanity and recovery (chapter 4), and the
writing on the wall during a banquet of Belshazzar, the supposed successor of Nebuchadnezzar (chapter 5) intend to
thrust home the message that God is the ultimate director of
history and that the arrogant who flourish must be brought
low. Thus the stories of the first half of the Book of Daniel are
staged outside of Palestine and contain no apparent reference
to the rueful condition under Antiochus' persecution in Palestine. Many scholars hence are of the opinion that the first half
of the book is older than the second (the second half was written in the second century B.C.). The author of the second half
connected the old tales of the righteous man, Daniel, with the

pious ones (including the author himself) of his day. He, describing the tyrant of the past, also envisaged the fearful oppressor Antiochus.

The second half of the book (chapters 7–12) consists of four visions concerning a dramatic consummation of the history of the ungodly empires (Babylonia, Media, Persia, Greece); then the everlasting world is given to the pious ones. The apocalyptic description of history by the author becomes increasingly detailed as the time period approaches his own era under Antiochus' persecution. In chapter 8 this tyrant is symbolized by "a little horn" which desecrates the sanctuary and the law and destroys "the people of the saints" but "shall be broken by no human hand."

The author further discloses the secret of the end-history by saying that the daily temple worship will be resumed after "two thousand and three hundred evenings and mornings," i.e., three years and two months after Antiochus' desecration of the temple in 168 B.C., which falls during the rededication of the temple by Judas Maccabeus in 165 B.C. A similar timetable is presented in chapter 9. The angel Gabriel explains to Daniel the hidden meaning of Jeremiah's prophecy of the seventy-year desolation of Jerusalem (Jer. 25:11; 29:10) in such a way that the "seventy years" indicates "seventy weeks of years," viz., four hundred and ninety years, which would bring them to the reign of Antiochus IV, who "shall come to his end with none to help him" (11:45). Consequently, the time of trouble precedes the final arrival of salvation, when the "many of those who sleep in the dust of the earth shall awake, some to everlasting life, and some to shame and everlasting contempt" (12:2). Therefore, the author urges pious sufferers to endure and "go your way till the end; and you shall rest, and shall stand in your allotted place at the end of the days" (12:13). The Book of Daniel is not just an apocalyptic crossword puzzle, but is indeed a book of encouragement during a time of terrible affliction.

QUESTIONS FOR DISCUSSION

1. What was the condition of the homeland when the exiled Jews returned?

2. How do you interpret the apparent conflict in their teachings concerning the temple between such prophets as Amos, Hosea, and Jeremiah on the one hand and Haggai and Zechariah on the other?

3. There are some Jews in contemporary society who do not accept the modern state of Israel on the basis of their belief that the reconstruction of the Jewish state is to be done only by the God-sent Messiah. Is their position justified from the biblical point of view?

4. Why did Ezra and Nehemiah prohibit mixed marriages so strictly? Was this prohibition always stressed throughout Israel's history? Should such a stern stance be applied to our society where the rate of religious intermarriage has been steadily increasing?

5. What were the major sects of Judaism? What were their characteristics? How is contemporary Judaism related to any of these ancient sects?

6. How was Jewish messianism developed? How is such messianic expectation alive among the Jews today?

7. What is the theological basis for the biblical eschatology?

8. What is the purpose of the Book of Daniel? Is the author's eschatological idea to be accepted as a source for contemporary belief in the expectation of the imminent end of history, or is it to be interpreted only in its own historical context? Is there any other alternative approach to this question?

Chapter Five

POETRY AND WISDOM

Despite a series of oppressive historical events, the exilic and post-exilic periods together formed a rather creative era. Not only were there such prominent prophetic voices as Ezekiel and Second Isaiah that generated messianic eschatology and apocalypticism, but there was also the establishment of the theocratic community itself. Another productive result of this era was the compilation of the books of Psalms, Job, Proverbs, Song of Solomon, Ruth, and Ecclesiastes as well as post-exilic historical works (Ezra, Nehemiah, and Chronicles). These books plus Daniel and Lamentations comprised the third division in the Hebrew Bible (the Kethubim, i.e., the Writings or Hagiographa) alongside the Torah (the Law) and the Nebiim (historical and prophetical books). Let us then examine these writings of the third division.

1. THE BOOK OF PSALMS

Throughout the ages, people of every religion have often expressed their religious feeling and perception in lyrics. Ancient Israel also left us poetry of considerable variety. In fact, one-third of the Hebrew Bible consists of poetic material. The Book of Psalms is a collection of their religious poems which proffer Israel's confession of faith in God in times of glory, crisis and sorrow. Pius Drijvers says, "In short, the whole of the Old Testament is reflected in the psalms."[1]

These psalms arose in the worship of God. Some of the poems can be dated to the pre-exilic time, but many of them are the product of the post-exilic community. The book as a whole has its setting in the liturgical practice of the second temple era, a practice that can be traced back to the pre-exilic period.

There are several collections recognizable in the Book of Psalms. The first collection (Pss. 3–41), whose superscription connects it with King David, is apparently the earliest section, though this fact does not necessarily mean that this section comes directly from David. The second collection (42–89), often called the Elohistic psalter because of its consistent use of *elohim* ("God" in Hebrew), is added to the first. It includes several sub-sections attributed to some temple singers (Korah and Asaph). Psalms 90–150 are eventually added. Psalms 1 and 2 function as an introduction. The authors of the psalms are unknown; the psalms arose and grew organically in worship through many generations and reached their final compilation in the late post-exilic period.

The literary format of our present psalms consists of five books: (1) 1–41; (2) 42–72; (3) 73–89; (4) 90–106; (5) 107–150. Each division ends with a doxology, except (5) where Psalm 150 serves as a final doxology. Such a format certainly is patterned after the five-book structure of the Torah.

Scholars have attempted closer examinations of individual psalms by analyzing their literary types:

(a) Laudatory psalms which praise God's majestic sovereignty in nature (8; 19:1–6; 93; 104; etc.)—for example:

The heavens are telling the glory of God,
and the firmament proclaims his handiwork (19:1).

Laudatory psalms also praise God's sovereignty in Israel's history (77; 135; etc.)—for example:

Thou art the God who workest wonders,
who hast manifested thy might among the peoples.
Thou didst with thy arm redeem thy people,
the sons of Jacob and Joseph (77:14–15).

(b) Thanksgiving psalms which resemble hymns in theme and literary form, offer thanks individually and communally to God for his salvation (30; 92; 107; 116; etc.)—for example:

I will extol thee, O Lord,
for thou hast drawn me up,
and hast not let my foes rejoice over me (30:1).

(c) Laments, individual in nature, comprise approximately one-third of the psalms. They express an outcry to God for help from dire straits (3; 5–7; 25–28; etc.)—for example:

O Lord, rebuke me not in thy anger,
nor chasten me in thy wrath . . . (6:1).

In cultic context, however, an "individual" sometimes represents also a congregation. (See, for example, Psalm 44 where "I" and "we" are used interchangeably.)

On the other hand, there are about ten psalms of lament that are explicitly collective by nature (i.e., the subject is "we"). These were composed on such occasions as the menace of a foreign enemy (e.g., 83), profanation of the temple (e.g., 74), the destruction of Jerusalem and the country (e.g., 79), and the exile (e.g., 137)—for example:

By the waters of Babylon,
there we sat down and wept,
when we remembered Zion. . . .
How shall we sing the Lord's song in a foreign
    land? . . .

Let my tongue cleave to the roof of my mouth,
if I do not remember you,
if I do not set Jerusalem
above my highest joy! (137:1, 4, 6).

The Book of Lamentations is not a part of the Psalms, but
since it represents an excellent example of a Hebrew lament,
we find it appropriate to make mention of it here. The book
consists of five poems portraying grief over the fall of Jerusalem in 587 B.C. It possesses various literary forms, including
the funeral dirge, and individual and communal laments. The
poems' trenchant description of the catastrophe persuades us
to believe that the date of composition is shortly after 587 B.C.

The first four poems (and possibly even the fifth) seem to
have originated from one single author, of whom little is
known, although tradition has without justification assumed
Jeremiah to be the composer. The book has been used in liturgy from ancient times by Jews to commemorate the loss of
Zion, and by Christians to commemorate the suffering of Jesus.

(d) Liturgical psalms are those which clearly indicate
their cultic use: sacrificial rite (e.g., 66), pilgrimage (e.g., 122),
song of Zion (e.g., 18; 46), and procession (e.g., 24). For example, 24:9–10 well indicates the liturgical procession at the temple gate:

Lift up your heads, O gates!
and be lifted up, O ancient doors!
that the King of hosts may come in.
Who is this King of glory?
The Lord of hosts,
he is the King of glory!

(e) Royal psalms are classified not only by literary characteristic but also by the content which commemorates the
king's enthronement (2; 72; 110), marriage (45), thanksgiving
for victory in war (18; 21), and pleas for the safety and victory
of the king (20). In Ps. 2:7, for example, we read the divine de-

cree of the enthronement of a king by means of his being adopted as God's son (this divine kingship ideology was the result of Canaanite influence).

(f) Wisdom psalms include didactic sayings (1; 37; etc.)— for example:

> Blessed is the man
> who walks not in the counsel of the wicked,
> nor stands in the way of sinners,
> nor sits in the seat of scoffers (1:1).

The Book of Psalms was, as Christoph Barth calls it, "the hymnbook and prayer book of the Old Testament church."[2] From Old Testament times, both Jews and Christians have cherished the book in their worship of God. Jesus himself often recited passages of the psalms; he and his disciples sang them together (e.g., Mk. 14:26), and, in fact, his last words on the cross, according to the Gospel writers, were taken from Psalm 22:1 ("My God, my God, why hast thou forsaken me?"). Early Christians regularly used the psalms in their common worship (1 Cor. 14:26) and sang them during imprisonment (Acts 16:25) as well as on joyous occasions (Jas. 5:13).

In the fourth century A.D., St. Ambrose inaugurated the practice of chanting the psalms by choir in the Western Church. It later became a Christian liturgical tradition to recite the entire aggregate of psalms at least once a week. Throughout the ages up until present days, the psalms have been and remain the heart of the Church's prayer book. They furnish prayers, private as well as public, with abundant vocabulary, images, and a source of inspiration.

2. WISDOM

Alongside the priestly and prophetic traditions, the wisdom tradition constituted the third major element of ancient Israel's religion. It produced several significant books of the Old Testament such as Proverbs, Job, Ecclesiastes, and the deutero-canonical wisdom literature, Ecclesiasticus and Wisdom of Solomon. The wisdom tradition is also found in such stories as the narrative of Joseph (Gen. 37–50), and in some portions of the prophetical books such as Amos, Isaiah, and others. The Books of Daniel, Jonah, and Esther also show traces of the wisdom heritage.

Unlike the priests with their cultic preoccupation and the prophets with their proclamation of God's Word, wisdom teachers were concerned with instructing the people about a life of propriety (discipline, moderation, hard work, tactfulness, etc.) by using often succinct and practical illustrations with a touch of poignancy and humor—for example:

> Like a gold ring in a swine's snout
> is a beautiful woman without discretion (Prov.
>   11:22).
> He who meddles in a quarrel not his own
> is like one who takes a passing dog by the ears
>   (Prov. 26:17).

According to Israel's wisdom, human life was unthinkable without God. Therefore, as G. von Rad says, "wisdom stands or falls according to the right attitude of man to God."[3] In other words, all this extremely practical counsel and mundane advice that the sages provided stemmed ultimately from reverence and loyalty to God, who was the source of wisdom.

> The fear of the Lord is the beginning of knowledge
>   (Prov. 1:7).
> All the ways of a man are pure in his own eyes,
> but the Lord weighs the spirit.
> Commit your work to the Lord,
> and your plans will be established (Prov. 16:2–3).

The "fear" of the Lord does not mean some psychical or physical feeling in the face of a threat; it is rather an "obedience to the divine will"[4] with a profound sense of awe. Hebrew sages possessed a relentless belief in God's sovereignty. God would reward the pious and punish the wavering, and it was human duty to submit to the divine dispensation.

Not only in such personal matters but also in the law and order of the universe was the will of the unfathomable God revealed. Consequently, the sages underscored the creatorship of God.

> The Lord by wisdom founded the earth;
> by understanding he established the heavens;
> by his knowledge the deep broke forth,
> and the clouds drop down the dew (Prov. 3:19–20).

One who created the whole world would rule that which happened therein. God as the Creator and God as the retributor are concepts closely interwoven in wisdom teaching; belief in God as Creator buttressed a faith in God as dispensator.

As the sages repeatedly affirmed in praise, this cosmos was the marvelous handiwork of God, a spendid manifestation of his wisdom. From this exaltation, the divine wisdom was described in poetic fashion as a person in and of itself, even somehow as an assistant in the creative work (Prov. 8; Job 28).

> When he [God] assigned to the sea its limit,
> so that the waters might not transgress his
>   command,
> when he marked out the foundations of the earth,
> then I [wisdom] was beside him, like a master
>   workman;
> And I was daily his delight,
> rejoicing before him always,
> rejoicing in his inhabited world
> and delighting in the sons of men (Prov. 8:29–31).

Such a personification of wisdom was most likely a result of the influence of other religions of the ancient Near East where a goddess of wisdom such as Maat or Ishtar was widely adored. In Israel, personified wisdom never became a second God, a cohort of Yahweh. Yahweh was the only deity who was worshiped exclusively.

God was utterly inscrutable, but his mystery was to be sought after through wisdom. Human reason was a gift of God; it was a human responsibility to use it to discover God's way in life. However, it was beyond human reach to fully comprehend God's way. Such a sense of human limitation and frailty led wisdom writers of a later time, such as the authors of Ecclesiastes and chapter 28 of Job, to embrace skepticism.

> But where shall wisdom be found?
> And where is the place of understanding?
> Man does not know the way to it,
> and it is not found in the land of the living (Job
>   28:12–13).

The origin of Israel's wisdom tradition is shrouded in mystery. It appears to have shared common features with the wisdom movements of the ancient Near East. Examples of such a similarity are found not only in the above-mentioned idea of the personification of wisdom but also in specific biblical passages such as Proverbs 22:17–23:14 which offer a close parallel to the Egyptian wisdom, the teaching of Amen-em-ope. However, "in Israel, wisdom never acquires the cultic or divinatory quality that typifies Mesopotamian wisdom, nor does it have the aristocratic tone of Egyptian wisdom."[5]

Israel's wisdom tradition was developed and preserved in such diverse settings as the royal court and local clans. In 1 Kings 4:29–34, King Solomon is said to have been noted for his wisdom and succeeding kings to have kept wisdom teachers as royal counselors. There may have been also scribal schools where wisdom was taught. In local clans, elders gave instructions to youngsters concerning practical and religious matters.

After Old Testament times, Jewish rabbis inherited the role of custodian of the wisdom tradition for their community. The New Testament writers saw in Jesus not only a true teacher (Mt. 12:42, etc.) but a manifestation of God's wisdom itself (Mt. 11:19; Col. 2:3).They also believed that God's wisdom was revealed through the Church (Eph. 3:10).

3. THE BOOK OF PROVERBS

This is a collection of wisdom sayings that were composed from the tenth to the fourth century B.C., although the superscription (1:1) ascribes the book to King Solomon. There is no general agreement among scholars as to the authorship of the book; some name learned scribes in the royal court or in schools, and others simply point to an educated social class. Whichever the provenance may have been, the book developed by stages over numerous generations down to the fourth century B.C. when it was completed.

The composite nature of this book can be observed in the fact that there are several different collections:

(1) Introduction (1–9)
(2) "The proverbs of Solomon," first collection (10:1–22:16)
(3) "The saying of the wise," first collection (22:17–24:22)
(4) "The saying of the wise," second collection (24:23–34)
(5) "The proverbs of Solomon," second collection (25:1–29:27)
(6) "The words of Agur" (30)
(7) "The words of Lemuel" (31:1–9)
(8) Sayings concerning the good wife (31:10–31)

The units (1) through (5) comprise the major part of the book, and of these, (2), which consists largely of mundane sayings, is generally considered to be the oldest (pre-exilic), while (1) is the latest (perhaps fourth century B.C.) and contains moral and religious sayings including the teaching of the personified wisdom.

4. THE BOOK OF JOB

A more dramatic representation of Hebrew wisdom is the Book of Job. This book consists of a prose framework (1–2; 42:7–17) and the poetic discourses (3:1–42:6). As many scholars contend, the former came from a pre-exilic story of a righteous man who was restored after a series of misfortunes, while the latter was composed either during or not long after the exile on the theme of theodicy (i.e., discussion concerning why the almighty and righteous God would allow evil to exist).

Chapters 1–2 set the stage of the whole story: Satan challenges the integrity of the righteous man Job ("Does Job fear God for nought?" in 1:9). God allows Satan to test Job. Here is a rare appearance by Satan in the canonical books of the Old Testament. He is not described as the devil, a traditionally familiar figure in the West, but rather as a divine attendant who functions as a prosecutor. Satan inflicts on Job a sequence of calamities: loss of property, the death of his children, and a loathsome disease. Nonetheless he maintains his righteousness.

Shall we receive good at the hand of God
and shall we not receive evil? (2:10).

Thereupon three friends of Job come to comfort him but instead end in dispute with him (2:11–31:40). They insist on the teaching of retribution against Job's claim of self-integrity. The teaching of retribution is a familiar one as it is stressed by the Deuteronomist and Proverbs. For example, the statement of Eliphaz, one of three friends, in 5:17 ("Behold, happy is the man whom God reproves; therefore despise not the chastening of the Almighty") occurs in slightly different form in Proverbs 3:11. Yet Job himself never yields to this ready-made answer as to his suffering and keeps asking the meaning of the horrible reality. He even professes: "I know my Redeemer [Vindicator] lives and at last he will stand upon the earth" (19:25). Job is seeking desperately ultimate vindication at God's hand rather than accepting any human explanation.

It is often the case that people in a difficult plight fall into cursing or utter despair, and that people at ease fall back upon a doctrine of platitudes. The reality of human suffering remains an enigma. No theory can readily explain it away. Is God cruel or simply absent? However, even suffering has meaning if human life itself is meaningful, says Viktor Frankl after the dreadful experience of the Nazi holocaust. It is the task of each individual to search for meaning. In fact, it is that obstinacy in search of the answer that makes Job a man of integrity.

The Book of Job, in fact, does not offer any clear-cut answer to the question of theodicy. Even in God's speech (38–41), the author tenders no new teaching except reaffirming the unfathomable nature of God. The author rejects any easy answer to the problem, but seeks its ultimate solution in a living encounter with the boundless God. The Book of Job is the story of the pilgrimage of a genuine soul who finds no rest but in the Eternal One. Job's restoration in the epilogue (42:10–17) symbolizes that final rest.

5. ECCLESIASTES

Though purportedly a reigning son of David—i.e., Solomon (1:1)—the author of this book must be a Jewish sage who lived in Jerusalem in the third century B.C. This view is supported by the linguistic features and ideas found in the book.

After various experiences in life, the author states, "All is vanity and a striving after wind" (1:14). Job's cynicism concerning the traditional teaching of retribution resonates here even more loudly. Human labor, knowledge, fame, wealth, etc. will lead one nowhere. Such skepticism, however, does not end in hedonism, since it also is empty. All creatures, including persons, "are from the dust and all return to the dust again" (3:20). There is no use in struggling, because "for everything there is a season . . . a time to be born, and a time to die. . . ." (3:1–9). Ecclesiastes is unique in the Old Testament above all for its characteristically down-to-earth attitude toward life and the world.

The sage's pessimism nonetheless does not end in total resignation. He insists on the importance of life; no matter what, there is still a life to live, which is the "portion" that God has given to each individual (3:22, etc.). It is human destiny and privilege to make the best of our "portion" and enjoy it to the fullest.

> He who joined with all the living has hope,
> for a living dog is better than a dead lion (9:4).

Just as Job, the author of Ecclesiastes contemplates seriously the painful reality of this world. Here he poses a "no-nonsense" stance in the midst of his sincere search, and in his own manner witnesses to a life of faith in God.

6. THE BOOK OF JONAH

Although the Book of Jonah is found among the prophetic books in the Old Testament, it is, in reality, not like other prophetic books at all, but a didactic story whose protagonist is the prophet Jonah. Jonah is mentioned in 2 Kings 14:25 as an eighth century prophet, but this story is not an historical account of his activity.

In the story, Jonah receives God's command to go to Nineveh, the Assyrian capital, to declare divine judgment, but he, out of fear, attempts to avoid the mission by sailing to Tarshish (Spain), only to be stopped by God with a storm and a large fish. He is thus compelled to go to the city to prophesy its destruction. But to his great surprise, a massive repentance of the Ninevites takes place. And instead of doom, God accepts their conversion. The unfulfilled prophecy disturbs Jonah immensely, but God instructs him of his mercy toward numerous lives in this big city by using an example of the life of a plant.

Scholars have often construed that the story was written in order to contest the Jewish nationalistic particularism of Ezra-Nehemiah's time by underscoring God's universal mercy.

However, the book betrays no such unequivocal intention. It rather teaches the importance of repentance. The gist of the story is, in fact, that the pagan Ninevites are spared from destruction through their repentance, whereas Jonah, who does not repent, receives a lesson from God. Recent scholars increasingly ascribe the date of the book's composition to approximately 500 B.C., a period when the need for contrite repentance was felt necessary as a result of sincere reflection upon the traumatic experience of the Babylonian exile.

7. THE BOOK OF RUTH

This book is, like Jonah, a didactic short story which narrates an episode of a pious and loyal woman, Ruth, in pastoral scenes. Upon the death of her husband, Ruth, a young woman from the land of Moab (east of the Dead Sea), kept an amicable fidelty to the Israelite family into which she married. She and her mother-in-law, Naomi, also a widow, returned to Bethlehem, the hometown of Naomi and her husband. Here Ruth met and married Boaz, a wealthy relative of Naomi's deceased husband. The marriage came about not only because of a mutual love between the two but also because of adherence to the ancient law called the levirate law, which required the nearest kin of the deceased (in the order of proximity of relationship) to marry his widow and preserve the name and property.

Scholars, again as in the case of Jonah, have often regarded the aim of this story to counteract the rigorous measures against intermarriage of the Jews and the Gentiles at the time of Ezra and Nehemiah. The story connects this foreign-born woman with the line of King David (4:17). This reference to David, however, is clearly a later editorial addition. The main thrust of the story seems rather to instruct readers about the hidden guidance of God by showing an unexpected development in the life of Ruth. It belongs to the same literary category as the story of Joseph, which demonstrates an identical theme by unfolding a series of unexpected occurrences in Joseph's life (Gen. 37–50). Consequently, recent scholars tend to date the story in the earlier monarchical period.

8. THE BOOK OF ESTHER

In contrast to the "universalistic" books of Jonah and Ruth, the Book of Esther tenders a nationalistic tenor by describing the Jews' deliverance from persecution in the Persian empire through the efforts of Esther and her uncle, Mordecai. Esther, a beautiful Jewess, becomes a queen by marrying Xerxes (the biblical Ahasuerus), king of Persia, and Mordecai uncovers a plot against the king's life, but he also incurs the hatred of the prime minister, Haman, by refusing to bow before him. The enraged Haman plans a pogrom. At Mordecai's appeal, Esther successfully intercedes with the king on behalf of the Jews and avenges Haman. The Jews are allowed by the king to annihilate their enemies, and Mordecai, for saving the king's life, attains a high rank in the country. To commemorate the whole event, the book ordains the feast of Purim.

The real intention of the story is to legitimatize the celebration of a feast already popular among the Jews in Mesopotamia and Persia, since the feast is not mentioned in the Torah and is most likely of pagan origin. The nucleus of the story was perhaps in existence during the Persian period but developed to its present form in the early Greek period by an unknown writer.

Like the stories of Jonah, Ruth, and Joseph, this tale of Esther and Mordecai is also entertaining. However, the latter conveys a less evident religious overtone, though it affirms a divine protective hand over the Jews of the diaspora (i.e., Jews who are dispersed outside Palestine). Later additions in the Septuagint (Greek translation at the end of the second century B.C.) supply a more pious vein, perhaps to offset the lack of religiosity in the Hebrew original.

QUESTIONS FOR DISCUSSION

1. Choose one of the following psalms—8, 23, 51, 104, 121, 132—and determine its literary type, structure, and message.

2. What did the Hebrew sages mean by "the fear of the Lord"? How does this meaning differ from or resemble the modern usage of this phrase?

3. What would you do in Job's place? Do you feel God is cruel, indifferent, or absent when people suffer?

4. What is, according to Ecclesiastes, the meaning of life? How does this view compare with that of other biblical authors?

5. What is the major thrust of Jonah?

6. What are the thematical differences and similarities between Ruth and Esther?

7. To what extent is the loyalty to the family and nation that is underscored in Ruth and Esther obsolete today? Or does it have validity now? If so, in what way?

8. Do the Old Testament writers always praise women's gentle submission to men?

Chapter Six

THE RELATIONSHIP BETWEEN THE OLD AND NEW TESTAMENT

1. THE OLD TESTAMENT AS WITNESS TO FAITH IN GOD

Through our study of the Old Testament books in all of the preceding chapters, it has become clear that the Old Testament is a collection of the writings of ancient Israel which, in greatly diversified ways, witnesses to her faith in God. Israel perceives the presence of God in the meaning of certain historical events (e.g., the exodus). The priests are guardians of the law which reveals the righteous way that should be followed. The prophets proclaim God's will in history. The wisdom teachers give various instructions pertaining to the prudent life. All these teachings strive to open people's eyes that they may see themselves and the world from God's perspective.

Thus according to the biblical view, the world is not a completely self-sufficient entity, but is open to a transcendent dimension. Our history likewise is not totally a self-contained mechanical process, but it owes its meaning and aim ultimately to God. The biblical writers urge us to perceive wonders and mystery in the world about us and also in our daily life. As Albert Einstein said, those to whom such an experience of mystery is a stranger are the same as the dead. God is the ultimate source of awe, wonder, mystery, meaning, and purpose for the whole universe. Faith in God means openness toward that source, and that openness indicates a willingness to explore, hope, accept, and live by it.

2. BELIEF IN YAHWEH

Ancient Israel confesses such a faith in Yahweh. Consequently, the center of the Old Testament as a record of that faith is Yahweh—the only God. The monotheism is, in fact, the most distinctive feature of the biblical religion. Nowhere else in the history of human civilization do we find such a persistent belief in one God. He is a transcendent God who, unlike the deities of Israel's neighbors, for instance, cannot be equated with any powers of nature. The transcendent nature of God, nonetheless, does not simply indicate his remoteness or otherness. It means also his full immanence; because he is "above" us, he is "within" us—he is truly all-embracing. God's transcendence is a supreme paradox.

Ancient Israel believes that this one and only transcendent God, the ultimate source of life (the Creator), chooses her as an instrument for revealing his salvific intention to the world (his covenant with Israel). Despite Israel's repeated perfidy, God is loyal to his promise of loving-kindness toward her (salvation). This faith not only endures a series of tragic historical events, but it further blossoms in the awareness of Israel's mission to the whole world and in eschatological messianism. Consequently, in Israel monotheism is not a subject of philosophical theory, but an historical experience. God reveals himself in the human mind as it participates in the process of history. The people of God confess that God is the only ultimate source of meaning and purpose of history. In this very sense, he is the God of history.

3. TIES BETWEEN THE OLD AND NEW TESTAMENTS

This selfsame faith in God is the fountainhead of both Judaism and Christianity. These two religions are undoubtedly sister religions. Attempts to sever the connection between the two by denying the Israelite/Jewish background of Christianity prove utterly abortive.[1] Both of them seek to worship the same God. The New Testament cannot be properly understood without the Old Testament.

In fact, there are several aspects of particular importance that indicate the inseparable relationship between the Old and New Testaments.[2] First of all, there is an historical connection, i.e., John the Baptist, Mary, Joseph, Jesus, and his disciples are all Jews who believe in and follow the God of the Old Testament. The New Testament writers emphatically identify Yahweh with the God whom Jesus calls Father, and they deem the followers of Jesus Christ as the new Israel, the people of God, a continuation of the old Israel. They revere the Old Testament as their Scripture, many passages of which they believe are to be directly applied to their Christian faith and situation. There are, moreover, numerous references to Jewish customs, traditions, laws, etc., some of which are of great significance. In fact, Jesus himself declares: "Think not that I have come to abolish the law and the prophets; I have come not to abolish them but to fulfill them" (Mt. 5:17).

Second, the New Testament reveals a scriptural dependence; quotations, allusions, etc., from the Old Testament lie in profusion in the New Testament. (Nestle-Aland's Greek New Testament marks two hundred and fifty-seven passages as being explicit citations.) For example, the well-known commandment of love which Jesus gives as the most important of all laws is quoted from the Old Testament ("love for God" from Deut. 6:5 and "love for neighbor as yourself" from Lev. 19:18). Furthermore, almost every key word of the New Testament is derived from the Old Testament vocabulary. Therefore, manifold concepts significant in the New Testament cannot possibly be clarified without their Old Testament roots.

Third, there are many corresponding theological themes between the two Testaments such as faith, creation, eschatological hope, love, promise, sin, judgment, forgiveness, salvation, righteousness, covenant, and so forth.

Fourth, Christians see the relationship of promise-fulfillment between the two Testaments. That is, the Old Testament tells of divine promise and hope for divine salvation, and the New Testament presents Jesus Christ as the fulfillment of that promise and the Savior. This does not, however, automatically signify that the concrete historical reality of Jesus is literally predicted in the Old Testament. Such a mechanical and superficial way of associating certain Old Testament passages with Jesus not only proves otiose, but tends to minimize the radical novelty of the person and mission of Jesus as the Christ. Rather, the New Testament writers recognize in Jesus Christ a culmination of the development of the Old Testament religion.

Finally, the Old and New Testaments are united in one and the same history of God's plan of salvation as perceived by the biblical writers. Both Testaments profess that God is not like a deistic god, a "perfect watchmaker," but is the God who loves and cares for the whole world despite human selfishness and disloyalty. World history is, therefore, an arena of his salvific acts—calling, reaching, and embracing us. His approach to us is indirect by way of a mediator, a subtle influence, rather than as a tyrant dealing with people as if they were robots to be dominated. The Bible, therefore, describes God as a loving parent or spouse who regards human free will and emotion. We have observed this fact in various Old Testament narratives, as with the patriarchs, Moses, the exodus experience, the settlement in the promised land, the judges, David, Jerusalem as the chosen place for special divine blessing, foreign threats as divine chastisement, worship in the temple, priests, prophets, the Babylonian exile, foreign king as the divine saving agent, the restoration of the homeland, the suffering servant of God, the Messiah, wisdom teachings and many other examples.

In the New Testament, there is one supreme Mediator,

that is, Jesus Christ, through whom God accomplishes his saving intention. After Jesus' crucifixion, history still continues to unfold to the end. As the Old Testament looks forward to the consummation, so does the New Testament; both are open to the future—a full manifestation of God's presence. This will be the time when every stray sheep and prodigal son will return home and the whole universe will find its final rest in the bosom of the all-embracing God.

QUESTIONS FOR DISCUSSION

1. Comment on the statement: "The God of the Old Testament is always angry, while the God of the New Testament is always loving."

2. In what way does the Christian Church need the Old Testament?

3. Why is the idea of mediatorship so important in the Bible? Do contemporary people need a mediator or medium between God and themselves?

Part II

THE NEW TESTAMENT

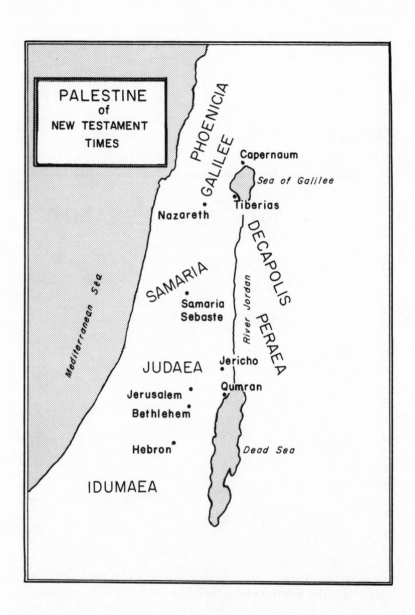

PALESTINE
of
NEW TESTAMENT
TIMES

PHOENICIA

GALILEE

Capernaum

Sea of Galilee

Nazareth

Tiberias

DECAPOLIS

Mediterranean Sea

SAMARIA

Samaria
Sebaste

River Jordan

PERAEA

JUDAEA

Jericho

Jerusalem

Qumran

Bethlehem

Hebron

Dead Sea

IDUMAEA

Chapter One

THE BACKGROUND
OF THE NEW TESTAMENT

1. HISTORICAL BACKGROUND

The Herodian Dynasty

The New Testament era began around the time of the death of Herod the Great (4 B.C.). Following the instruction of Herod's will, the Roman emperor Augustus divided Herod's country into two halves; he appointed Archelaus, Herod's son, as ethnarch over half (Judaea, Idumea, and Samaria), and split the other half further into two in order to name the other two sons of Herod as rulers. He placed Antipas as the tetrarch over Galilee and Peraea, and Philip as the tetrarch over Batanaea, Trachonitis, Auranitis, and other small provinces. However, Archelaus proved incompetent; he was accused of brutal treatment toward the Jews and was banished to Gaul in A.D. 6. His territory was reduced to a province under direct Roman rule by a procurator.

Antipas divorced his wife to marry Herodias, his brother's wife. John the Baptist violently denounced this irregular marriage, which incurred the ruler's wrath, and thus John was executed. Antipas faced a fate similar to Archelaus when he was

banished to Lyon in Gaul in A.D. 39 on some damning charge
by Agrippa I. By contrast, Philip was successful as a ruler; he
was popular and his reign was peaceful. He died childless in
A.D. 34. His territory was given to Agrippa I, who later pro-
cured Judaea and Samaria as well; as a result he ruled over
the identical land once ruled by Herod the Great, his grandfather. After his reign (A.D. 41–44), the land was governed by
Roman procurators (A.D. 44–66). Eventually Agrippa II succeeded his father, remaining so loyal to Rome that he even
fought against the Jewish revolt on the side of the Roman
troops. With his death (ca. A.D. 100), Herod's dynasty ceased
to exist.

The Jews and the Romans

The relationship between the Jews and Romans, though
varied from time to time, was tense from the moment of the
Roman arrival in Palestine in 63 B.C. Among the Jews, there
were those who curried favor with Rome and prospered by be-
coming part of the Roman power structure ("Herodians" in
the Gospels), and some who were considered Jewish traitors,
while there were others who did not hesitate to take up weap-
ons against Rome. A representative group of these militants
were the Zealots. Between these extremes were many other
dissatisfied groups. Rebellion was always simmering near the
surface.

There were no less than fourteen procurators sent to Jerusalem between the time of Herod's death and the Jewish up-
rising against the Romans in A.D. 66. With few exceptions,
these officials utterly failed in their administration by making
wrong judgments and committing savage cruelty; they had no
comprehension of the Jewish people's tenacious adherence to
the ancestral religious tradition and of their resistance to Hellenistic civil and religious customs. For example, Pontius Pilate (A.D. 26–36), before whom Jesus stood trial, appropriated
temple funds for the construction of an aqueduct. When the
Jews protested with outrage, he responded with relentless
force. On another occasion, it was charged that his troops

heartlessly cut down defenseless Samaritans; this charge finally resulted in his dismissal.

Consequently, the tension between the Romans and the Jews mounted steadily under the procurators. An increasing number of Jews were drawn into militant groups such as the Zealots. The Jews, however, were not unified; there was a wide range of differing views and positions not only between militants and moderates (those of some means and security) but also within these two groups themselves. Numerous acts of brutality were aimed at compatriots as well as acts of revengeful violence against the Romans. By the time of the last procurator, Florus (A.D. 64–66), open fighting had become common, and the organized revolt against Rome finally broke out (A.D. 66) when Florus crucified many of those who protested against his plundering of the temple treasury.

This "First Jewish Revolt," fought in the spirit of the Maccabeans, was easily suppressed by the Roman generals Vespasian and Titus; Jerusalem fell and the temple was burned in A.D. 70. Thousands of the Jews were slaughtered, crucified, or deported to the slave markets of the empire. (The fate of Christians in Jerusalem is not clear, but the Church historian Eusebius stated in the fourth century A.D. that they fled from Jerusalem to Pella in Transjordan prior to the destruction of the city.)[1]

Thenceforth Judaism became a religion without a temple, priesthood, sacrificial rites, or homeland (until 1947). Instead it centered around the synagogue (house of prayer) and the rabbi (teacher); the law remained its heart. Among the various Jewish sects, the one which survived was the Pharisees, and consequently rabbinic-Pharisaic Judaism became the sole ancestor of Judaic tradition down to our modern day.

2. SOURCES OF THE HISTORICAL JESUS

What do we know about the life of Jesus who was born into these discouraging times? Is there evidence pertaining to the historical Jesus in ancient Roman and Jewish sources in addition to the New Testament itself? From the Roman side, some references were made by Tacitus and Suetonius. The former stated in his *Annals,* xv, 44 (written in A.D. 112–113) that Christ was executed by Pontius Pilate and was the founder of the Christian sect which was later under persecution by Nero. Suetonius mentioned in his *Lives of the Caesars* (ca. A.D. 121) disturbances in the Jewish community in Rome under Claudius (A.D. 41–54) resulting from Christian preaching.

As for the Jewish sources, Josephus' *Antiquities,* xviii, 3, 3 refers to Jesus' crucifixion by Pilate. The Talmud (a massive compilation of ancient Jewish commentaries and interpretative writings) contains occasional references to Jesus which are polemically biased, yet they cannot be ignored. All of these references to Jesus are, however, penurious and imprecise,

HISTORICAL CHART OF NEW TESTAMENT TIME

B.C.	63	The Romans take Jerusalem
	37–4	Herod the Great
	7–4?	Birth of Jesus
A.D.	27–29?	Activity of John the Baptist
	29–33?	Ministry of Jesus
	30–33?	Crucifixion
	33–35?	Conversion of Paul
	50?	1 Thessalonians
	53–54?	Galatians
	53–54?	Paul's Corinthian correspondence, Philippians
	55–56?	Romans
	56–58?	Philemon
	70	Fall of Jerusalem
	71–73?	Mark
	70's	2 Thessalonians, Colossians, Ephesians
	80's	Matthew, Luke-Acts
	90?	Council of Jamnia
	90's	Hebrews, 1 Peter, Revelation
	ca. 100	John, Catholic Letters, James, Pastoral Letters
	ca. 125	2 Peter
	132–135	War with the Romans

compelling us to seek information germane to Jesus from the New Testament, especially the Gospels.

3. WHAT ARE THE GOSPELS?

The word "gospel" (from old English "god-spel," i.e., "good story") is a translation of the Greek word *euangelion* meaning "good news." It occurs four times in Matthew in reference to the message of Jesus, while it is also used to designate the whole ministry of Jesus as Mark 1:1 indicates. From the second century onward, it has come to signify also these four writings about Jesus Christ: Matthew, Mark, Luke, and John.

The Historical Jesus

Not only does the word "gospel" have nothing to do with biography, but the content of the Gospels does not present an objective description of the life of Jesus. To begin with, the four Gospels leave out much of Jesus' life. Mark and John are utterly mute on the subject of his career until his baptism by John the Baptist. Matthew and Luke relate the birth story (in which they differ on some points), and Luke also briefly mentions a story of Jesus' visit to the Jerusalem temple at the age of twelve. Yet, otherwise, they are silent about his life until his baptism. According to Luke 3:23, "Jesus, when he began his ministry, was about thirty years of age." This statement is opaque; "thirty" may simply allude to the fact of adulthood. It is John who mentions three successive Passovers in Jesus' public life (2:13, 23; 6:4; 13:1), which indicates that his ministry lasted three years. But no such information is even hinted at in the first three Gospels. In fact, it could have been a much shorter ministry, for the Fourth Gospel is so theologically motivated that it may not really carry historical accuracy (discussion of this question will follow later).

Moreover, a peculiar fact is that all four Gospel writers devote considerable portions of their writings to the final week of Jesus' career; Mark spends six out of his sixteen chapters, Matthew eight of twenty-eight, Luke six of twenty-four, and John ten of twenty-one. Such a disproportionate literary construction causes some scholars to regard the Gospels as "passion narratives with extended introduction."[2] It is thus clear that the Gospels intend to describe, more emphatically than anything else, the message that "the Christ suffered and entered into his glory" (Lk 24:26).

The Kerygmatic Christ

The next issue of major significance is the fact that none of the four Gospel writers claims to have been an eyewitness to the events which he describes. As will be discussed in the next section, the Gospel writers relied extensively on older sources. The initial passage of Luke typically deliniates this fact:

> Inasmuch as many have undertaken to compile a narrative of the things which have been accomplished among us, just as they were delivered to us by those who from the beginning were eyewitnesses and ministers of the word, it seemed good to me also, having followed all things closely for some time past, to write an orderly account for you, most excellent Theophilus, that you may know the truth concerning the things of which you have been informed (Luke 1:1–4).

Each of the Gospel writers edited traditional sources about Jesus according to his own theological concern which arose from the situation of the community to which he belonged. In other words, the Gospels were historical and communal products of early Christians; they met, heard, believed, and remembered Jesus the Christ, and orally passed the stories of their experiences of him to others, who in turn orally transmitted these stories further. Finally, it was Mark who first compiled these oral traditions and produced a written document (ca. A.D. 70), which has been called the Gospel According to Mark. Matthew and Luke used Mark's Gospel alongside other sources to write their Gospels. (See the next section for a discussion of this question.)

The Gospel narratives evolve around the central message

of Jesus as the Christ (from the Greek *christos,* "Anointed," i.e., Messiah). It follows that the Gospels are essentially confessions of faith of the early Church. That is to say, the content of the Gospels consists of what the early Church acknowledged as significant for its faith. Consequently, it is hardly possible to go beyond the experience and confession of the early Christian community to the original events. A distinguished New Testament scholar, G. Bornkamm, states at the beginning of his well-known book *Jesus of Nazareth:* "No one is any longer in the position to write a life of Jesus."[3]

From the foregoing consideration, we have come to the conclusion that the portrait of Jesus which we find in the Gospels is not exactly that of the historical Jesus but the figure perceived and professed by the early Church, i.e., Jesus the Christ as the one it proclaimed—the kerygmatic Christ as scholars call him ("kerygma" is the Greek word often used in the New Testament meaning "proclamation"). The kerygmatic Christ is, therefore, a theologically reflected concept of the post-Easter Christian community. To be sure, the historical Jesus and the kerygmatic Christ are not two entirely separate entities, since the latter would not have come to exist without the former. In order to describe their relationship, we may picture two concentric circles: the inner circle represents the historical Jesus and the outer circle the kerygmatic Christ. When we readers look at it, we see only the kerygmatic Christ, and it is extremely arduous to reach to the historical Jesus. Yet he is there. In fact, results of the form-critical and redaction-historical analyses by recent scholars point to the fact that the teaching of the kingdom of God, the parables, and the Lord's Prayer must have come undoubtedly from the mouth of Jesus.[4]

4. SOURCES OF THE SYNOPTIC GOSPELS

The Synoptic Gospels

Even a cursory reading of the four Gospels reveals the existence of close and extensive parallels among the first three as against the independent nature of the fourth. In fact, only about nine percent of the material of the three Gospels coincides with material in the fourth; they differ in the order of events, literary style, the content and method of Jesus' teaching, and the writers' theological views. To give some striking examples, according to the first three Gospels Jesus made only one journey to Jerusalem, whereas the Fourth Gospel records several visits to the capital during his public ministry. Again according to the former, Jesus held his Last Supper, which was a Passover meal, and then was crucified on the fifteenth of Nisan (the first month of the ancient Jewish calendar which falls in March or April in our calendar), but in John's narrative he died one day earlier (cf. John 18:28; 19:14).

Mark's Priority

Matthew, Mark, and Luke share similar structure, content, and wording. Approximately ninety-one percent of Mark is paralled in one of the other two Gospels or in both, and the same can be said of about fifty percent of Matthew and about forty percent of Luke. Because of this fact, these Gospels are called "the Synoptic Gospels" ("synoptic" came from the Greek word *synoptikos,* "common view"), i.e., they present a common perspective concerning Jesus.

From the statistical computation mentioned above emerges the assumption that Matthew and Luke used Mark's Gospel as a main literary source. They even depended upon Mark's language and word choice. In fact, when Matthew and Luke agree with each other, they also coincide with Mark. Furthermore, when they differ from each other, they also diverge from Mark. There are also many cases where Matthew and Luke appear to have altered Mark's passages with the intention of producing better and smoother reading and of tendering their own theological views. (Compare, for example, Jesus' commandment of love in Mark 12:28–34 with Matthew 22:34–40 and Luke 10:25–28.) Consequently, a great majority of contemporary scholars are convinced of the priority of Mark.

Q and Special Sources

Matthew and Luke used another common source as well. There are over two hundred verses which they share in common but which are not found in Mark. These comprise almost one-third of Matthew and one-fourth of Luke. Moreover, they primarily consist of the sayings of Jesus with a heavy emphasis on eschatology. Scholars, therefore, postulate the existence of a collection of Jesus' discourses that were available to Matthew and Luke. The date of this collection was approximately as early as A.D. 50. This source is referred to as Q—the initial of the German word *Quelle* meaning "source."

In addition to Mark and Q, Matthew and Luke contain material which is unique to each of them. To explain this fact, scholars assume that Matthew and Luke appropriated oral traditions circulating in the early Church. Those special sources are usually referred to as M and L respectively. An example of M is found in some sections of the Sermon on the Mount (Mt. 5:17–22, 27–29, 33–37, etc.), and a well-known example unique to L is the parable of the prodigal son (Lk. 15:11–32).

Consequently, the sources of the Synoptic Gospels can be put as follows:

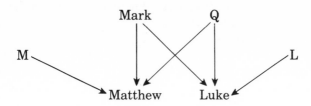

The Synoptic Gospels thus complement one another with highly composite literary sources and theological views. Some modern authors have compared them to a television set which ultimately shows a picture on the screen resulting from many sources via a complicated electric mechanism inside. The Gospels feature the stories of Jesus the Christ. Let us then watch what Mark has to present.

QUESTIONS FOR DISCUSSION

1. In what social condition was Jesus born? Compared to ours, in what ways was it different or similar?

2. Is Jesus meaningful only in such a situation as Palestine of the first century A.D.?

3. How much do we know about the historical Jesus? What evidence do we have? Is it clear? If not, does this jeopardize in any way the credibility of Christianity?

4. What does the concept of the "kerygmatic Christ" mean? Is this belief a crucial basis of Christianity?

5. Why did the ancient Christians include four Gospels in the New Testament canon instead of a single one?

6. What are the Synoptic sources? How did these sources come to exist?

7. Compare the Lord's Prayer in Matthew 6:9–15 and Luke 11:2–4. Explain the differences.

Chapter Two

THE GOSPELS

1. THE GOSPEL ACCORDING TO MARK

Traditionally the writer of the Second Gospel has been identified with John Mark mentioned in Acts and a few other writings of the New Testament, for some of the Church Fathers of the second century A.D. (e.g., Papias and Irenaeus) state that this Mark was involved as an "interpreter of Peter" in writing about Jesus Christ. This identification, however, is uncertain; there exists no evidence in the New Testament which bears out this assertion. For the sake of convenience, we call the author of this Gospel Mark.

Likewise, no clear indication is available as to the date of the Gospel's composition. Scholars usually assume it to have been written shortly after A.D. 70 when Jerusalem was destroyed by Romans. The place of composition is also vague; ancient tradition and its modern followers associate it with Rome, but many other contemporary scholars name Galilee. The writer might have been among non-Jewish Christians outside Palestine, since he occasionally explains some Jewish customs, translates Aramaic words, and uses Latin expressions (cf. 4:21; 5:9; 6:37; 7:4; 12:14; 15:39, etc.).

The literary structure of Mark's Gospel is as follows:

(1) Introduction (John the Baptist and Jesus' preparation for ministry): 1:1–13
(2) Ministry in and near Galilee: 1:14–8:26
(3) Prelude to the passion in Jerusalem: 8:27–10:52
(4) Jesus in Jerusalem: 11:1–16:8 (16:9–20 is a later addition)

Mark's Gospel is not simply a collection of disparate short stories concerning Jesus but instead a rather well integrated entity with a deliberate literary plan moving from the beginning of Jesus' ministry in Galilee through the expansion of his work outside Galilee and in Jerusalem, concluding with the passion, death and resurrection. Such a chronological and geographical framework seems cogently to serve the purpose of presenting Mark's theological intentions. What then are the characteristic messages of this Gospel?

Proclamation of God's Reign

A leading theme of Mark's Gospel is the imminent manifestation of God's reign, which is Jesus' central message itself: "The time is fulfilled, and the kingdom of God is at hand; repent and believe in the Gospel" (1:15). What then is the kingdom of God? It is not a territorial entity; Jesus shows absolutely no political ambition. It rather indicates the active reign or rule of God, and therefore it is "neither a spatial nor a static concept; it is a dynamic concept."[1]

This concept is already quite dominant in the Old Testament; Yahweh is believed to be the true and ultimate ruler who exercises lordship over the world with justice and love. In Jewish apocalypticism, the notion is accentuated by highly dualistic and eschatological overtones. That is, the opposition between God's rule and this-worldly powers, and also between future glory and present misery, is placed in sharper focus (cf. Dan. 4:34, 44).

God's reign in Mark's Gospel stands in the same spiritual trajectory; it is an eminently apocalyptic symbol. This symbol exercises its dynamism by demanding decision-making: Which do you follow, the transient power of this world or the eternal reign of God? According to Mark 1:15 cited above, God's reign is imminent but has not quite yet come. Nevertheless, it is not said to be a future reality unrelated to the present. It is rather vitally connected with the here and now. The moment people choose God's reign, they find themselves in its midst. Therefore, in Jesus' proclamation in Mark 1:15, "the fullness of time," "the kingdom of God," "repentance," and "believe in the Gospel" are uttered in one breath. The kingdom of God is not a heavenly Camelot or fanciful Shangri-la. It is a reality of life living in the will of God with joy. In Mark, not only Jesus' teachings but also his works (healing, exorcism, crucifixion) are all oriented to the theme of God's reign. Jesus as the Messiah (Christ), Mark testifies, has proclaimed and indeed brought it to us.

If God's reign indicates such a dynamic reality of life, then it must involve the actual process of living such a life. In fact, Mark records Jesus' parable where God's reign, described as a growing reality, is compared to a grain of mustard seed which grows up to "the greatest of all shrubs" (4:30–32). The reign of God will develop to its consummation. This is depicted in Mark 13 in a typically apocalyptic way: the arrival of "the Son of Man" on the clouds with great power and glory following a universal catastrophe. The time of this "end" is determined only by God, yet it is imminent. Such tense expectation of the apocalyptic end, as modern scholars suggest, was occasioned in the turbulent situation immediately after the fall of Jerusalem in A.D. 70.

The Messianic Secret

This teaching of God's reign, in Mark's Gospel, is revealed gradually by Jesus, first to his disciples, then to other people, and finally to everyone through the crucifixion. That is to say, the identity of Jesus is kept secret from the public until the last moment of his earthly life. In 4:11 we read that Jesus says to his disciples that "the secret of the kingdom of God" has been given only to them, while to others "everything is in parable." He strictly orders that his messiahship and his works should not be openly disclosed (cf. 1:34, 43; 3:12; 5:43; 7:36; 8:30; 9:9). It is Peter's confession that first professes Jesus as Messiah (Christ) in Mark's Gospel (8:27–30). Up until this point, Jesus is known as a wonder-worker, a rabbi, a prophet, etc., but from this point on, the crucial meaning of his messiahship begins to unveil, i.e., his ministry in Galilee ends and his final messianic mission in Jerusalem—passion, death, resurrection—commences. At this juncture also, Jesus tells his disciples explicitly about his final destiny for the first time. Thus Peter's confession constitutes a pivotal point at the middle of this Gospel.

The public manifestation of the secret is postponed until the Jewish high priest pointedly asks him at the trial, and he identifies himself as "the Christ, the Son of the Blessed" (14:61–62). Finally, this identification is confirmed by the Roman centurion at the foot of the cross as Jesus breathes his last: "Truly this man was the Son of God!" (15:39). Such a progressive unveiling of the hidden Messiah is uniquely found in Mark. The theme of "the messianic secret" is indeed the unifying motif of Mark's Gospel. By using this motif, the author strives to describe that not only is Jesus the eschatological messenger who brings to the world the good news but he himself is the reality of God's reign at the end time. Let us then consider further Mark's understanding of Jesus.

The Son of God

In Mark's Gospel, as in the other Gospels, Jesus is sometimes called the Son of God. In the Old Testament, the whole nation of Israel is referred to as the children of God (Ex. 4:22, etc.), the righteous ones within Israel (Hos. 1:10, etc.), angelic beings (Gen. 6:2; Job 1:6), David (2 Sam. 7:14), and an anointed king (Ps. 2:7). The last of these passages is of particular significance, since it is quoted in Mark 1:11 (Jesus' baptism). In both passages, the idea expressed is of a legal relationship of adoption by God, and not a physical sonship of the Godhead (which is a Hellenistic notion). In Mark's Gospel as a whole, neither a physical nor a metaphysical sense is attached to this appellation ascribed to Jesus. The "Son of God" is used rather as a messianic title, and it also connotes love and filial obedience to God the Father.

This connotation is further corroborated by Jesus' use of the term "Abba" in addressing God. According to a renowned German scholar, J. Jeremias,[2] there is no single example of God being addressed as Abba both in the Old Testament and in Judaism, although the idea of God's Fatherhood can be found. Jesus, by contrast, always called God Abba in his prayers (except in Mk. 15:34, which is a quotation from Ps. 22:2). Abba was originally a young child's word used in everyday talk (and that is perhaps the reason why ancient rabbis avoided it in addressing God). Jeremias maintains that such a complete novelty and uniqueness of Abba in Jesus' use indicates "the heart of Jesus' relationship to God," confidence, security, reverence, and obedience. It was a sacred word to Jesus, and he taught it to his disciples accordingly.

Sigmund Freud psychologically construed the Fatherhood of God in terms of the so-called Oedipus complex and returned the verdict that it expressed a neurosis.[3] Recent feminists have claimed that it is a symbol of male chauvinism that causes alienation, and that it is exigent for modern Christians to come up with a more dynamic symbol for God than this old, anthropomorphic symbol of Father.[4] In opposition to these negative arguments, R. Hammerton-Kelly in his recent book contends that God's Fatherhood means, as exemplified in the exodus event (cf. Ex. 4:22–23), freedom from human bondage and freedom for a loving relationship with God predicated upon faith rather than on fate.[5]

Although the concept of the Fatherhood of God was born and nurtured throughout centuries in decidedly male-dominated societies, it seems difficult for us to replace it with some other term such as "parent" which, though more neutral, is more impersonal. Thus God as the Father is still too significant a symbol to simply discard, as the idea is so dearly expressed in Jesus' use of the innocent child's greeting, Abba. Indeed, God's Fatherhood indicates an eternal family of love centered around God, which transcends and fulfills the transient family of this world. Therefore, it really is beyond sexist prejudice. After all, God is, as the Old Testament bears witness, a-sexual, i.e., above human sexuality (including androgyny) without denying sexuality itself.

The Son of Man

This appellation ascribed to Jesus occurs rather frequently in Mark as well as in Matthew and Luke in the sayings of Jesus. It refers to (1) his activity on earth, (2) his suffering, death, and resurrection, and (3) the exalted heavenly figure who will come in glory from heaven. In these references an image of a Messiah is presented—the Messiah, who has authority to forgive sins, heal sickness, and exorcise, has a special divine mission of suffering and resurrection, and is to return soon.

Such a messianic connotation of the Son of Man is also found in ancient Jewish tradition. The reference to the "the Son of Man coming in clouds with great power and glory" (Mk. 13:26; Mt. 24:30; Lk. 21:27) is from Daniel's apocalyptic vision where "one like a Son of Man" came to God and was given "dominion and glory and kingdom" (Dan. 7:13–14). In Daniel's passage, the Son of Man is a collective figure representing the people of God (the pious Jews), but there is evidence, though not pre-Christian, that it was interpreted as a Messiah in some Jewish apocalyptic literature (cf. 1 Enoch 37–71 and 2 Esdras 13). Consequently, we may conclude that the Son of Man is an apocalyptic title for Messiah that was applied to Jesus by early Christians. (Modern scholars' opinion varies as to whether or not Jesus used the term for himself.)

Furthermore, Mark seems to claim that Jesus was the suffering servant of the Lord prophesied in Isaiah 53, for it is said in Mark 10:45 that the Son of Man came to "give his life as a ransom for many." Jesus, by dying a vicarious death, accomplished his mission as a crucified Messiah. But the Christian story of Jesus does not end there; it rather begins at this very point, for the crucifixion is a supreme manifestation of divine love. In this very act of self-giving, Jesus discloses "the unprecedented and incomprehensible incarnate love of God" (E. Schweizer).[6] For this reason, the crucifixion already anticipates the resurrection—the conquest of death and new life. We have observed in Genesis 3 that human sin is described as a severance of relationship with God, which means "death." What is achieved by Jesus' resurrection is that the severance caused by human beings is now overcome, and that, as a result, they are reconciled to God and alienation is eradicated. Christians, therefore, call it "at-one-ment"—atonement. The divine love (all-unifying dynamism) accomplishes it all.

E. Schweizer contends that Mark wrote his Gospel in order to preserve the memory of what Jesus said and did which revealed that divine love, thereby correcting other views of Jesus which were in existence in his day such as the idea of Jesus simply as a rabbi, as a wonder-worker, or as a heavenly visitant. The intention of this Gospel writer went beyond a simple Christological presentation; it strove to encourage readers to stay firm in the divine love that Jesus manifested, living through hardships of persecution with the apocalyptic hope for the imminent eschaton.

2. THE GOSPEL ACCORDING TO MATTHEW

Traditionally this Gospel has been considered to have been written by Matthew, one of the twelve disciples of Jesus, who was originally a tax collector in Galilee (Mt. 9:9; he is called "Levi" in Mark 2:14 and Luke 5:27). This identification, though ancient (e.g., Ignatius and Origen of the second century A.D.), is not sustained by the New Testament itself, where there is nothing to suggest the personal identity of the writer. The very fact that the writer used Mark's Gospel and the Q source well indicates that he was probably not a direct companion of Jesus.

The use of Mark also points to the date of composition of the Gospel after A.D. 70. It is a matter of conjecture how much later than 70; many modern scholars ascribe it to the late eighties. The author seemingly was intimate with Jewish customs and practices, and was writing his Gospel in Greek apparently for Jewish Christians. It follows that he was most likely among Hellenized Jews. Some scholars thus suggest that the place of composition might have been Syria (Antioch?). It is not at all clear, however.

Scholars' views as to the structure of the Gospel are divided. Some of them analyze it as having five major blocks, each consisting of narratives and teachings, punctuated by the phrase "and when Jesus finished . . ." (7:28; 11:1; 13:53; 19:1; 26:1). These major blocks are sandwiched between the introduction (infancy narrative in chapters 1–2) and the epilogue (crucifixion and resurrection in chapters 26–28).[7] However, other scholars see three divisions: (1) the person of Jesus (1:1–4:16), (2) the proclamation of Jesus (4:17–16:20), and (3) the crucifixion and resurrection (16:21–28:20).[8] The phrase "from that time Jesus began" marks the beginning of the second and third divisions.

According to the former analysis, the structure of the Gospel intimates the five-book pattern of the Torah, which suggests Jesus as a new Moses who gave a new law. It is true that in Matthew's theology the law constitutes a vital component, but it is not a new law (cf. 5:17–20), and Jesus is present as a true teacher of God's will, not a new law-giver. The alleged five-book structure is not that clearly detected either. The latter analysis has the advantage of underscoring the passion, death, and resurrection of Jesus—undoubtedly the culmination of Jesus' career. The theme of Jesus the Messiah emerges more clearly from this view as well.

Jesus, the Long-Awaited Messiah

Perhaps the most prominent theological theme of Matthew is that Jesus is the Messiah whom Israel (and the whole world) expected. Matthew underscores this theme more strongly than any other New Testament writer. This fact is seen, for example, in that Matthew cites Old Testament passages more often than the others; there are forty-one quotations in his Gospel, of which twenty-one are common to Mark and Luke (i.e., evidently Mark is the source), and ten of the rest (twenty) are found in no other New Testament book. These quotations are often followed by the formula, "that it might be fulfilled . . ." or something similar. Thus the intention on the part of the writer is crystal clear: he strives to prove that the life of Jesus fulfilled what the Old Testament had prophesied.

With such a theological intention, Matthew begins his Gospel with a long genealogical list which traces Jesus' lineage from Abraham via David to Joseph, the husband of Mary. That is to say, this theological genealogy asserts that Jesus was a genuine Israelite from the house of David. Jesus' birth story is a direct continuation of the same theological intent. The main thrust of the story reposes in his name; the writer explains the meaning of the name Jesus (in Hebrew "Yehoshuah," Joshua, meaning "Yahweh saves") by stating: "You shall call his name Jesus, for he will save his people from their sins" (1:21). Then a quotation from the Old Testament (Is. 7:14) immediately follows. In this quotation, too, a name is crucial; the "son" is to be called "Immanuel," which means "God with us."

The next Christmas episode in Matthew is the visit of the magi from the East (2:1–12). The crux is again identical here. The magi, representing the Gentiles, pay homage to a messianic king by presenting gifts accorded to a royal figure at Bethlehem, the birthplace of King David (cf. Mt. 2:5–6; Mi. 5:2). This true king of peace is contrasted with the bloodthirsty tyrant Herod in 2:13–18. All these stories point to Jesus as the long-awaited Messiah from the royal house of David. This legitimizes the person and mission of Jesus, and also demonstrates God's plan of salvation in history.

The theme that the Messiah fulfilled the Scriptures finds its various expressions further in Matthew. The writer explains Jesus' healing ministry in the context of his redemptive mission. It is stated in 8:17: "This was to fulfill what was spoken by the prophet Isaiah, 'He took our iniquities and bore our diseases.'" In other words, according to Matthew, Jesus healed the sick not for the sake of performing miracles but as a step in his vicarious suffering and death as the suffering servant of God. This healing-redemptive mission of the Messiah culminated in his crucifixion (cf. 20:28; 26:28). In Matthew's understanding, healing and salvation are virtually identical. Hence Jesus declared to his Pharisaic critics, "But if it is by the Spirit of God that I cast out demons, then the kingdom of God has come upon you" (12:28). By bringing "God's kingdom" to the people, he was fulfilling God's salvific intention in history.

Fulfillment of the Scriptures

It is Matthew, not the other Gospel writers, who records Jesus' words in 22:34–40 that "all the law and the prophets" depend upon the two commandments: "Love your God" (Deut. 6:5) and "Love your neighbor as yourself" (Lev. 19:18). This is a radical interpretation of the law and the prophets, i.e., love fulfills them all. Although Jesus forcefully asserted: "Think not that I have come to abolish the law and the prophets; I have come not to abolish them but to fulfill them. For truly, I say to you, till heaven and earth pass away, not an iota, not a dot, will pass from the law until all is accomplished" (5:17–18; this passage is unique to Matthew), he was not a slavish or mechanical legalist. He actualized the spirit of the law.

Hence, for example, he did not hesitate to help and heal people on the sabbath, the day of rest, though the law prohibited work. He declared to his Pharisaic accusers: "The Son of man is lord of the sabbath" (12:8). The heart of the law was love, and as Matthew tells us, Jesus actually accomplished it by showing genuine love for God and for people. This characteristic theme of Matthew, "to fulfill the Scriptures," therefore, must mean "to bring them into actualization."[9] Jesus actualized what was intended by the law and the prophets by performing God's will with the utmost obedience.

As the fulfiller of the Scriptures, Jesus is, according to Matthew, the authoritative interpreter of the law. Jesus "taught them as one who had authority, and not as their scribes" (7:29). As noted previously, Jesus' discourse and teaching material dominate this Gospel, and teaching authority is considered to belong ultimately to the Messiah. As a matter of fact, Jesus is addressed as "teacher" about forty times in the Gospels. Beyond doubt, he was treated as a rabbi by the people.

However, he was someone more than a rabbi, for he did not initiate any rabbinic school as other noted rabbis (e.g., Hillel and Shammai) did. Matthew goes even further by identifying Jesus with God's wisdom in 11:19:

The Son of man came eating and drinking, and they say, "Behold, a glutton and a drunkard, a friend of tax collectors and sinners!" Yet wisdom is justified by her deeds.

Here we may very well see the Old Testament wisdom tradition which personifies the divine wisdom (cf. Prov. 8–9). Jesus the Messiah is thus the authoritative interpreter of the Scriptures because he is divine wisdom personified.

Because of such unique theological characteristics of Matthew's Gospel, modern scholars sometimes call it a "Jewish Christian Gospel" and the author a "Christian rabbi." Matthew argues against Jews (particularly the Pharisees), insisting on the authority of the Christian interpretation of the Scriptures on the one hand; on the other hand, he contends against some Gentile Christians by pointing out the importance of the law. It is understandable that the ancient Christian Church should place Matthew's Gospel at the very beginning of the New Testament, for it functions as a connecting point between the two Testaments by virtue of its dominant concern with the Old Testament and the Jewish background of the Christian Gospel.

The Church as the New Israel

Matthew (not Mark or Luke) emphatically states that Jesus came primarily for Israel's salvation (15:24) and that Jesus sent his disciples only to Israel (10:5–6). Israel, however, rejected Jesus, which, in Matthew's view, provided reason for the mission toward the Gentiles (cf. 21:43). Therefore, uniquely in Matthew, we read that the risen Jesus tells his disciples, "Go therefore and make disciples of all nations . . ." (28:19). Thus the old Israel was superseded by the Church of all nations; the Church is the new Israel—the true people of God.

Matthew's emphasis on the Church stems seemingly from historical factors as well. The apocalyptic impact which dominated earliest Christian thinking (as seen in the Q source, Mark's Gospel, and some of Paul's letters such as 1 Thessalonians) is altered by Matthew (though it did not disappear; cf. chapters 24–25). In lieu of the future consummation of history, the present reality of the Church as a more organized and enduring institution steps forward. In other words, the time of Matthew is already the age of a more entrenched Church, still awaiting patiently the second coming of Christ which has not arrived.

Consequently, Matthew closes his book by mentioning Jesus' words concerning the basic task of the Church, i.e., making disciples, baptizing them, and teaching them to observe all that Jesus commanded the disciples. These words conclude with: "Lo, I am with you always, to the close of the age" (28:20). This last message corresponds with the Christmas message at the beginning of this Gospel: the newborn baby is called "Immanuel" (God is with us). And this is Matthew's very basic message—Jesus is "God with us."

3. THE GOSPEL ACCORDING TO LUKE

In the opening statement (1:1–4), the author explains the aim and reason for writing this Gospel: (1) he wrote this book by using traditions (perhaps both oral and written) about Jesus Christ which had been "delivered" to the Christian community; (2) these traditions came from authoritative sources ("eyewitnesses and ministers of the word"), and therefore the book is reliable; (3) the author "followed all things closely (i.e., investigated)" and wrote "an orderly account" for the sake of the "most excellent Theophilus."

Consequently, the author was not a first-generation Christian, and his book was apparently meant to be more like literature (when compared to Mark and Matthew) for some prominent Roman official by the name of Theophilus to read. Moreover, according to Acts 1:1, the same author also produced the second volume for Theophilus (which is our "The Acts of the Apostles").

Since at least the second century A.D., this author has been identified as Luke, "a beloved physician," and a companion of Paul (Col. 4:14). This identification, however, is by no means conclusive; there is no definite evidence to support it.

The book's dedicatee, Theophilus, is totally unknown. The name itself was common among both Gentiles and Jews of those days. Some modern scholars conjecture that since the name means "friend of God," it might have been a cover-up name used to conceal some Roman official who was protective of the Christians during an era of persecution. Others surmise that Theophilus was not a specific individual but any "friend of God." The real identity of the person remains an enigma. The content of Luke-Acts betrays no particular trace as to the identity of the expected reader(s). However, the writer seems to presuppose a Gentile audience.

Many scholars date the Gospel sometime in the eighties A.D. because (1) it uses Mark as a basic source, (2) it reflects a very early stage of Gentile mission, and (3) it appears to have knowledge of the fall of Jerusalem in A.D. 70. The place of composition is unknown, but the Gospel shows its Hellenistic environment. It has a universalistic perspective (as we will discuss later), and it also avoids Semitic words (e.g., "skull" for "Golgotha" in 23:33). Luke shows less concern than Matthew about the theme of "Jesus as the Davidic Messiah." In contrast to Matthew's frequent use of "fulfillment," Luke prefers the expression "it is necessary" (*dei* in Greek). This Greek word occurs as often as forty-two times in Luke-Acts, and it is also used rather often in ancient Greek writings indicating an inevitable fate preordained by the deities. The idea expressed here is quite clear: Jesus' life and death were the destiny which God had set up for world history. Luke understands and presents Jesus from a Hellenistic intellectual milieu. He was most likely a Gentile Christian.

An outline of Luke's Gospel is as follows:

(1) Prologue: 1:1–4
(2) Introduction: 1:5–4:13
(3) The ministry in Galilee: 4:14–9:50
(4) The journey to Jerusalem: 9:51–19:44
(5) The ministry in Jerusalem: 19:45–21:38
(6) The passion and resurrection: 22:1–24:53

The History of Salvation

As we observed, according to the opening statement Luke writes his Gospel in an "orderly" manner. This order can mean an historical one, but it is not historical in the modern sense; a theological perspective, in fact, dominates the historical aspect. In this sense, Luke's writing, like that of Mark and Matthew, belongs to the category of "Gospels." Of vital significance to Luke's theological perspective is the idea of the history of salvation. It is Luke's fundamental conviction that God's salvation of the world develops throughout history—from the beginning to the end. This history of salvation unfolds through three phases: (1) the era of "the law and the prophets," (2) the time of Jesus, and (3) the era of the Church.[10]

(1) The era of "the law and the prophets" runs from the beginning of history to John the Baptist. This is the period of the anticipation and promise of the proclamation of the good news of the kingdom of God.

> The law and the prophets were until John; since then the good news of the kingdom of God is preached, and every one enters it violently (16:16).

Luke, like Matthew, presents a genealogy of Jesus, but the two genealogies do not exactly coincide. Luke traces the lineage, unlike Matthew, backward from Jesus even to Adam who, he says, is "of God" (3:38). While Matthew intends to prove that Jesus was an authentic Israelite from the house of David, Luke stresses the messianic claim of Jesus, not on the basis of descent, but on God's plan, and strives to present the significance of Jesus in the context of the whole of world history. Jesus' mission is to all mankind including Israel. We all are originally "of God" but have been lost. Jesus came to rescue all of us from alienation, bringing us back to God the Father. Thus, for example, Luke uniquely quotes Isaiah 40:4–5 which ends with: ". . . and all flesh shall see the salvation of God" (Lk. 3:6; cf. also 2:30–32). It is also Luke who repeats the theme that Jesus "came to seek that which was lost" (cf. 15:4, 32; 19:10, etc.).

Luke 1:5–38 presents credentials of Jesus the Messiah. This section includes the annunciation, births of John the Baptist and Jesus, the young boy Jesus in the temple, John's preaching, Jesus' genealogy, and Jesus' test in the wilderness. Each of these short literary units is intended to attest to the identity of Jesus as the Messiah, the Son of God. In Luke there is no such motif of the messianic secret as found characteristically in Mark. According to Luke, the appearance of John and Jesus was the explicit work of God's Spirit; John was "filled with the Holy Spirit even from his mother's womb" (1:15); his parents, Zechariah and Elizabeth, were also filled with the Holy Spirit (1:41, 67); Mary conceived through the Holy Spirit (1:35); the Holy Spirit descended on Jesus at his baptism (3:22; 4:1). Likewise, "led by the Spirit," Jesus was tested in the wilderness (4:1).

The Time of Jesus

This period begins when Jesus returned to Galilee "in the power of the Spirit" (4:14). Luke then mentions Jesus' ministry in Nazareth; at a synagogue he read Isaiah 61:1–2 and said, "Today this Scripture has been fulfilled in your hearing" (4:21). The Isaiah passage says that the Spirit of the Lord is upon the prophet to preach good news to the poor, to declare release to the captives, to recover sight to the blind, to set the oppressed at liberty, and to proclaim the acceptable year. According to Luke, Jesus identified himself with this prophet. Jesus' word "today" indicates the time of messianic salvation, rather than one particular day.

These great themes prescribed in Isaiah dominate Luke's narratives of Jesus. For example, only Luke tells us that the baby Jesus was laid in a manger "because there was no place in the inn" (2:7) and was visited by the shepherds from out in the fields. (By contrast, Matthew says that Jesus was born as "king" in the "house" and "worshiped" by the wise men who, led by the star, came from the East with the gift of precious treasures.) Furthermore, such merciful and humane stories as the parables of the Good Samaritan (10:30–37) and of the prodigal son (15:11–32) are found uniquely in Luke. Luke records Jesus' words, "Be merciful as your Father is merciful" (6:36), while Matthew puts: "Be perfect . . ." (5:48). Again only Luke reports that the penitent thief on the cross was forgiven (23:43). Luke's Gospel is indeed the Gospel of the poor and the oppressed.

Consequently, we may understand well Luke's message that the reign (kingdom) of God brought about by Jesus is a world of peace, justice, and love even here and now. We may also notice in Luke that such an expectation of the imminent end (eschaton) as expressed in Mark recedes into the background; instead we find the age of a Church in which the Spirit executes its power. Thus uniquely in Luke we read:

> The kingdom of God is not coming with signs to be observed; nor will they say, "Lo, here it is!" or "There!" For behold, the kingdom of God is in the midst of you (17:20–21).

Furthermore, there is a significant difference between Luke and Mark in the understanding of salvation through Jesus. Compare the following passages:

Luke 22:27	Mark 10:45
For which is greater, one who sits at table, or one who serves? Is it not the one who sits at table? But I [Jesus] am among you as one who serves.	For the Son of Man also came not to be served but to serve, and to give his life as a ransom for many.

While, for Mark, salvation was accomplished through Jesus'
suffering and death as a "ransom for many," for Luke these
acts were a supreme service for the world. Luke underscores
the fact that Jesus was and is a neighbor in the real and true
sense of the word; he is not only *with* the people but also always and genuinely *for* the people—one who has manifested
genuine love through life and death. Therefore God glorifies
him. In fact, Luke tells us more about Jesus' resurrection than
Mark and Matthew. Mark makes no mention of the appearance of the risen Jesus, and Matthew does so only once, while
Luke describes at least three occasions. Moreover, according
to Acts 1:3, Jesus appeared to his disciples "during forty days"
to speak about the kingdom of God until his ascension (glorification).

The Era of the Church

The descent of the Holy Spirit upon the disciples at Pentecost after Jesus' ascension (Acts 2:1–13) marks the beginning
of the third epoch of salvation history. God's Spirit generated
Christians, though few in number, to create a community of
common worship and fellowship.

Luke takes pains to relate this period to the time of Jesus
by presenting Jesus as a supreme model for Christians to follow. Jesus possessed a strong belief in God, resulting in utmost
obedience to God, and he also had a most genuine love for others. He prayed and attended worship services regularly. "So,
be like Jesus!"—this is the message. As Jesus was a witness to
God, Christians should become witnesses of the reign of God.
Writing about the crucifixion of Jesus during a difficult time
of persecution, Luke sees and draws a parallel between Jesus
and his followers. For example, just as Jesus said on the cross,
"Father, forgive them, for they know not what they do" (Lk.
23:34), Stephen uttered at his martyrdom, "Lord, do not hold
this sin against them" (Acts 7:60). The suffering of Christians
is, in fact, the suffering of Jesus (cf. Acts 9:4).

As Christians participate in Jesus' suffering, they also
take part in his glorification. There is always hope, Luke assures us, no matter how hard the reality may be. His intention

here is to make his readers acknowledge their role and position in salvation history, thereby continuing the life of witnessing. Luke's theological perspective is thus all-embracing in both the spatial and the temporal senses; God's salvation will reach the whole world and every nation, covering all of history. Salvation is not only being delivered from some specific sins or miseries but involves as well each individual's participation in that dynamic process of God's working in history.

4. THE GOSPEL ACCORDING TO JOHN

At least since the latter part of the second century A.D., this Gospel has been traditionally ascribed to John, the son of Zebedee, but it must have been written after the apostle's time, as it betrays rather clearly a later stage of the theological and historical development of the early Church. Modern scholars generally date the Gospel during the final years of the first century A.D.

Johannine Community

If the author was not the apostle John, then who was it? An important clue to the answer to this question is found in 19:35: "He who saw it [Jesus' crucifixion] has borne witness—his testimony is true, and he knows that he tells the truth—that you may also believe." Three parties are involved here: the eyewitness, the writer, and the reader. The eyewitness must be the "beloved disciple" mentioned in 19:26, and he must have been the teacher of this writer, who, in turn, was the teacher of the reader. They formed a kind of "community" or "school" which shared a common tradition about Jesus Christ—let's call it the "Johannine community."

Although the identity of the "beloved disciple," the ultimate source, is not known, it seems certain that the provenance of this Gospel can be traced back to the life and ministry of Jesus. This fact does not mean that the Gospel is a photographic record. Like the other Gospels, it is a confessional presentation of Jesus the Christ. In fact, John's Gospel manifests a highly unique theology of its own; it is much more explicitly theological than the Synoptic Gospels. In other words, it presents the theology of the "Johannine community."

Thus the Fourth Gospel, though sharing the same heritage, is quite independent of the Synoptics. It is uncertain whether or not the writer had access to the Synoptic sources, but even if he was acquainted with them, he apparently did not rely on them. In fact, ninety percent of the Synoptic material is simply not found in John.

What then motivated the author to write this Gospel? A once popular view was that John's Gospel represents a prominent stage in the Hellenization of early Christianity. However, recent scholarship increasingly underscores the Gospel's origin in a situation of conflict with "the Jews." (Notice that Jewish opponents are called so in a collective way and are no longer dealt with according to groups such as the Pharisees, the Sadducees, etc., as in the Synoptics. This fact indicates a clear separation of the Church and the synagogue.) That is to say, though the "Johannine community" originated in synagogues perhaps in Asia Minor, it became involved in a bitter controversy with fellow Jews as it accepted and began openly proclaiming Jesus as the Son of God and the Savior. It was eventually expelled from the synagogues. (Some references to the expulsion are found in 12:42; 16:2, etc.) Such a heated debate most likely occasioned John's Gospel; it was written in order to confess faith in the God who sent Jesus as the Savior, as is clearly stated at the closing:

Now Jesus did many other signs in the presence of the disciples, which are not written in this book; but these are written that you may believe that Jesus is the Christ, the Son of God, and that believing you may have life in his name (20:30–31).

Structure of John's Gospel

The structure of the Fourth Gospel is also somewhat different from that of the Synoptics. It opens with a poetic prologue (1:1–18) which announces Jesus Christ as the ultimate revealer of God. John the Baptist bears witness to this "Lamb of God, who takes away the sin of the world" (1:19–34). Unlike the Synoptics, the author, without mentioning the temptation story, immediately begins to narrate Jesus' call of his disciples (1:35–51) and then his public ministry. Jesus' ministry consists mainly of teaching and performing the seven miracles (2:1–12:50). Again unlike the Synoptics, John's Gospel contains neither parables (only a few brief allegories) nor exorcisms. There is no institution of the Eucharist at the Last Supper, but instead Jesus' washing of his disciples' feet is mentioned (chapter 13). Then a lengthy discourse of Jesus (chapters 14–16) and his prayer (chapter 17) follow. Chapters 18–20 describe the arrest, trial, crucifixion, and resurrection. Chapter 21, narrating the risen Jesus at the Sea of Galilee, is a later addition, which, however, also originated in the "Johannine community."

Johannine Christology

One of the striking contrasts between the Synoptics and John's Gospel is that in the former the central message of Jesus' preaching is God's reign, whereas in the latter Jesus speaks about himself. Jesus' self-pronouncements, uniquely found in John, are a typical example; they assume a fixed style: "I am . . ." (e.g., "I am the way, the truth, and the life" in 14:6). This style corresponds to that of God's self-revelation in the Old Testament (e.g., Ex. 3:6; Is. 41:4). The "I am" sayings of Jesus in the Fourth Gospel thus certainly intend to reveal the identity of Jesus as the divinely commissioned Messiah. Not only this literary formula but the whole context of the Gospel revolves around the question of who Jesus is.

This Gospel, in fact, opens with a declaration of the incarnation in Jesus as the "Word" that was "in the beginning with God" (1:2). It speaks of Jesus' eternal existence as the personified Wisdom mentioned in the Book of Proverbs. ("Word" and "wisdom" are often synonymous in ancient Judaism.) The purpose of the incarnation of this eternal "Word" is to bring to the world "grace and truth" (1:17). Jesus is the Son of God, who alone ultimately reveals God. He is also depicted in the Fourth Gospel as the heavenly Redeemer and eternal life-giver, unlike the apocalyptic Son of Man or the Jewish Messiah from Nazareth in the Synoptics.

This exultant Christology is expressed in various ways: the fiery preacher, John the Baptist, of the Synoptics is called simply the "voice" of a witness, and the miracles ("signs" in John's term) are done by Jesus to demonstrate the dignity of the Messiah rather than out of compassion or as a breaking through of the apocalyptic end, as in the Synoptics. In the same vein, the suffering and death of Jesus constitute a process of glorification in John unlike the acts of self-humiliation in the Synoptics. In fact, John draws a symbolic analogy between Jesus' "lifting up" on the cross and his exaltation (3:14; cf. also 14:28; 16:5, 28; 20:17). Moreover, this Gospel is the only writing in the New Testament which mentions Jesus as being addressed directly as God; doubting Thomas calls the risen Jesus "My Lord and my God" (20:28). The author also records Jesus' words: "I and the Father are one" (10:30).

The heightened Christology in John's Gospel is also presented in a characteristically dualistic context. Jesus is the true light descended from above to the dark world below. Those who believe and follow him can be born again into a new spiritual life by the death of the old self of "flesh." They can discover and love the truth and learn to hate falsehood, and will receive eternal life.

Such dualism in John has been explained in terms of an extraneous influence such as Gnosticism. Gnosticism was a religious movement widespread in the first three centuries A.D. Gnostics believed that although mankind lives in ignorance and illusion, one can attain spiritual liberation through divine knowledge (*gnosis* in Greek) by experiencing a fusion of the soul with the divine. Consequently, Gnosticism is highly dualistic; it underscores an essential conflict between the divine and this world and also between the innate immortal soul and the physical body, dominated by sensual passions. According to Gnosticism, a heavenly savior can release persons from such a bond by revealing this esoteric divine knowledge to liberate the inner soul.

Though the Fourth Gospel was written in such a cultural

and spiritual milieu and displays concepts noticeably resembling Gnostic ideas (e.g., heavenly redeemer, dualism, etc.), John's dualism is basically alien to that of Gnosticism. John, for example, affirms emphatically that this world was created and is loved by God and Christ. As R. Bultmann says,[11] it is a "dualism of decision," choosing to follow God in the historical reality, unlike Gnostic dualism where one is totally controlled by some cosmic powers. Such cosmic fatalism is entirely missing in John's Gospel.

Realized Eschatology

One of the distinctive messages of John's Gospel presents Jesus as the true life-giver; he is "a spring of water welling up to eternal life" (4:14), and "the bread of life" (6:35–51). Just as a branch, vitally connected with the vine, can live and bear fruit, people can live a true life if they abide in this life-source (15:1–6). Consequently, the "eternal life" in John is not primarily a matter for the future (beyond the end of this world), but is a crucial question of the here and now, since God has already achieved salvation through Jesus. This is clearly stated in 3:18: "He who believes in him is not condemned; he who does not believe is condemned already in the name of the only Son of God" (notice the tense). Likewise in 16:33: "I have overcome the world." And we read in 17:3: "And this is eternal life, that they know thee the only true God, and Jesus Christ whom thou has sent."

The decisive act of God's salvation, according to John, has already been actualized (although the second coming of Jesus is mentioned a few times). Such a theological assertion forms a characteristic contrast to Mark's expectation of the apocalyptic Son of Man; one underlines "already," while the other "not yet." Scholars have coined the term "realized eschatology" to express the Johannine view of eschatological salvation. To be sure, the "already" by no means points simply to the past of Jesus' life-death-resurrection, but it is vitally related to the life of Christians. As long as they abide in Christ, the "already" is a present reality. Therefore, for John, faith does not mean a belief in certain doctrine but a living and trustful communion with God through Christ. In this very sense, the Johannine teaching of eternal life corresponds to the Synoptic kingdom of God.

Paraclete and Agape

How can Christians have such communion after Jesus has departed from this earthly life? Does he remain with them simply in the tradition or memory concerning what he said or did? The author of the Fourth Gospel says that communion is possible through the Holy Spirit who is called the "counselor" (*parakletos* in Greek). The Spirit is with and in them (14:16), reminding them of all that Jesus said (14:26). The Paraclete is the Spirit of truth who bears witness to Jesus (15:26). Thus, the Spirit is a bond which unites Christians both with Jesus Christ and God the Father.

The dynamism of union is love (*agape* in Greek). This is a favorite term in John's Gospel (used thirty-one times in John, whereas in Matthew only seven times, in Mark five times, and in Luke ten times). Therefore, "abide in his love" (15:9) and "love one another" (13:34). The Fourth Gospel is hence often called the "Gospel of love."

QUESTIONS FOR DISCUSSION

1. What do the Gospel writers mean by "God's reign"? This reign is said to be "yet to come" and also "here and now." Is there an irreconcilable conflict between these two? What is the relevance of this concept in today's trouble-filled world?

2. Mark talks about Jesus being abandoned. Find examples of this. Is Jesus also abandoned in our society?

3. According to the early Christians, what is the meaning of the Fatherhood of God and the Sonship of Jesus? Are these antiquated metaphors?

4. According to the Synoptic Gospels, why did the Messiah have to be crucified?

5. Compare the ways in which the Synoptic writers describe Jesus' messiahship. Which of them do you feel is more easily related to present-day understanding?

6. Compare the theological intentions of Matthew and Luke in their genealogies of Jesus.

7. Compare the theological ideas detected in the birth story of Jesus in Matthew and Luke.

8. What is the meaning of the statement, "Jesus fulfilled the Old Testament"? Is a human "fulfillment" of the biblical command totally different from Jesus' work of fulfillment? Or is there any similarity?

9. Why did Luke adopt the particular vantage point of salvation history in his Gospel? How do we modern people fit in this theological scheme?

10. Why did John use a dualistic pattern in his writing? Can dualistic thinking affect our understanding of Jesus himself (i.e., was he a man, God, or both)? Can it provide us with an effective way of looking at our world?

11. What does "eternal life" mean in John? In what way can a person live "eternally"?

Chapter Three

THE ACTS OF THE APOSTLES

The Acts of the Apostles constitutes the second volume of work by Luke. Not only does Acts 1:1 state this fact, but there is no evidence to the contrary. Both books present a similarity in vocabulary, literary style, theological thought, method of organizing sources, purpose, and general pattern. Luke describes Jesus from his birth to his resurrection in the first volume, and from his ascension and the birth and growth of the Christian Church to Paul's journey to Rome in the second volume. Consequently, in the New Testament, Acts functions as a connecting bridge between the Gospels and the letters of Paul.

In Luke's thought, as we have observed already, salvation history plays a decisive role. Luke depicts in Acts the development of God's dealings with the world throughout the Church. Therefore, this book is not what we call history; it is, nonetheless, the only available source for the earliest stage of the history of the Church.

The author seems to be using various sources of oral and written material to write this volume as he did for his Gospel. But unlike what we find in the Gospel, it is rather difficult to distinguish the sources he appropriated; modern scholars' opinion varies considerably.[1] An abrupt shift of the subject

147

from the third person plural to the first person plural in 16:10 illustrates the use of different sources. The source which narrates Paul's missionary journeys in the first person plural (therefore often called the "we source") might have originated in a diary or the travel notes of a group of Paul's companions. The speeches of Stephen, Peter, and Paul also comprise a large bulk of the book (one-third); they are not exactly literal records, but are literary compositions based upon the preachings of the early Gentile churches.

Luke is said to have been a companion of Paul (Col. 4:14), but it is not at all clear how close they were, and "companion" does not necessarily mean disciple. In fact, their theological ideas sometimes disagree (e.g., concerning the law). By the time Luke wrote (perhaps in the late nineties A.D.) about Peter—the leading character in chapters 1–12—and Paul—the leading character in chapters 13–28—both of them had died a few decades earlier. Consequently, it is unlikely that Luke was always writing with a fresh memory or from exact sources.

The outline of Acts is as follows:

(1) Christians in Jerusalem: 1:1–8:1
(2) The spread of Christianity to Judaea and Samaria: 8:1–9:30
(3) The spread of Christianity to the Gentile world: 9:31–28:31

Christians in Jerusalem

This first section of Acts opens with the final teaching of the risen Jesus to his disciples:

> But you shall receive power when the Holy Spirit shall come upon you; and you shall be my witness in Jerusalem and in all Judaea and Samaria and to the end of the earth (1:8).

This statement by Jesus, in fact, presents the theme of the whole book. Notice that the emphasis is placed first on the dynamism of the Holy Spirit, second on the geographical spread

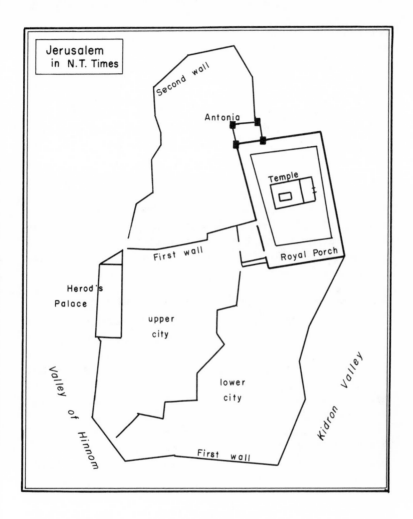

Jerusalem
in N.T. Times

Second wall

Antonia

Temple

First wall

Royal Porch

Herod's
Palace

upper
city

Valley of Hinnom

lower
city

Kidron Valley

First wall

of the Christian Gospel from Jerusalem to "the end of the earth," and third on the fact that the Christians are called "witnesses" of Jesus. All of these are characteristically Lukan ideas.

After choosing Matthias to replace Judas (1:15–26), the disciples received the Holy Spirit on the day of Pentecost (chapter 2). This Pentecostal experience is described to have been such an ecstatic one that they spoke in tongues, which cynical outsiders mockingly called drunkenness. Luke, in Peter's sermon, attempts to legitimize the experience by quoting the prophet Joel who said that God's Spirit would generate extraordinary events (Jl. 2:28–32). The descent of the Spirit, according to Luke, initiates the Church. The life of the earliest Church is summarily described in 2:43–47: the Christians "had all things in common," attended the temple together, and had "favor with all the people."

Thus, the Church, in Luke's narrative, was set in motion in Jerusalem. But it met violent opposition from Jews; the preaching and healing of John and Peter caused their arrest and trial (chapters 3–5). Despite the strict order of prohibition by Jewish authorities, the apostles continued their ministry. This set the stage for Stephen's sermon and martyrdom (chapters 6–7).

The Spread of Christianity to Judaea and Samaria

Stephen's martyrdom appears to have triggered great persecution against the church in Jerusalem, which destined the Christians to be "scattered throughout the region of Judaea and Samaria, except the apostles" (8:1). Luke thus opens his stories about the Christian mission to the world outside Jerusalem, and he also introduces "a young man named Saul" (later called Paul) into his writing at this juncture.

Luke records the conversion of Paul three times in Acts (9:1–30; 22:3–21; 26:9–23). According to these accounts, it took place when Paul was on his way to Damascus in Syria to persecute Christians there; in a visionary experience, he "heard a voice saying to him, 'Saul, Saul, why do you persecute me?' and he said, 'Who are you, Lord?' And he said, 'I am Jesus, whom you are persecuting' " (9:4–5). Paul realized that Jesus, who was crucified, dead and buried, was truly a living reality, and that the persecution he had done out of zeal for the law was actually a horrendous and vain defiance against the ineradicable truth (in Jesus' words in 26:14: "It hurts you to kick against the goad").

It is impossible for us to reconstruct or to objectively analyze such an extraordinary religious experience. All we know is the historical fact that a rabid persecutor suddenly became a fervent believer and a missionary to the Gentiles. This incident occurred sometime between A.D. 33 and 36, a few years after Jesus' crucifixion. (This "conversion" of Paul will be discussed further in the next chapter.)

The Spread of Christianity to the Gentile World

Luke reports in 9:32–11:18 that Peter played a significant role in the initial stages of the early Christian mission to the Gentiles; against Jewish Christians' criticism, he insisted that "to the Gentiles also God has granted repentance unto life" (11:18). So the stage was set for an overt attempt to reach out to the Gentile world, and thus a church was founded in Antioch of Syria (11:19–26). Luke mentions that "in Antioch the disciples were for the first time called Christians" (11:26). The origin and initial meaning of this designation are not certain, and it occurs only three times in the New Testament (Acts 11:26; 26:28; 1 Peter 4:16), which may well indicate its pagan provenance, possibly with some scornful implication. However it became fully accepted by the Church by the beginning of the second century A.D.

From chapter 13 to the end of the book, Luke narrates the Christian missionary movements among the Gentiles, in which Paul plays a key role. According to Luke, Paul made three missionary journeys (13:1–14:28; 15:36–18:22; 18:23–21:16). On the first journey, he and Barnabas sailed from Antioch to Cyprus, visited southern Asia Minor, and returned to Antioch.

Between the first and the second journeys, Paul went to Jerusalem to attend a council (15:1–35).[2] This council was held to discuss whether or not the Gentile Christians were also required to observe the practice of circumcision and to obey other Mosaic laws, as strongly urged by some converts from the Pharisaic party. It was decided, apparently under the moderatorship of Peter and James, to "lay upon them no greater burden than these necessary things," i.e., abstinence from meat sacrificed to idols, from blood, from meat of strangled animals, and from unchastity. This event seems to tell us of: (1) the central authority of the Jerusalem church led by Peter and James, (2) a victory of the Gentile Christians apparently represented by Paul, and (3) the official acceptance of the Gentile mission with the barrier of circumcision totally removed. From chapter 15 onward, Paul and the Gentile churches definitely become dominant, while the apostles and the Jewish Christians fade from view.

On the second journey, Paul, Silas, and Timothy visited the Christian communities in Syria and Cilicia, and then in the cities in Macedonia such as Philippi, Thessalonia, Beroea, and further on in Athens and Corinth. Then they went to Ephesus, from which they sailed to Caesarea in Palestine. The third journey of Paul originated at Antioch, covered the cities in Asia Minor and Greece, where he had visited previously, and ended in Jerusalem. The historical accuracy of these three itineraries is uncertain, and scholars often view the itinerary pattern as a literary device used by the author to organize his narratives concerning Paul's activities. Nonetheless, there is no doubt that Paul made extensive trips for several years in those regions to establish and encourage Christian communities, despite persistent opposition and persecution from both Jews and Gentiles.

The rest of the book (21:17–28:31) deals with Paul's deportation to Rome which was the result of a riot against him. In Jerusalem, Paul's presence, and also the charge that he had brought uncircumcised Greeks into the temple, precipitated a riot among the Jews. Upon Paul's appeal to Caesar as a Roman citizen, the Roman officials took him into protective custody and eventually deported him to Rome to stand trial. Acts ends with the account of his life of preaching in Rome while awaiting trial in a house of arrest. Ancient Christian tradition claims that Paul, after his release, continued his missionary work, traveling even as far as Spain, was arrested again, and was finally executed. There is no conclusive evidence to verify this legend, but it is most likely that he was executed in Rome during the persecution of Christians by the Roman emperor Nero in A.D. 65.[3]

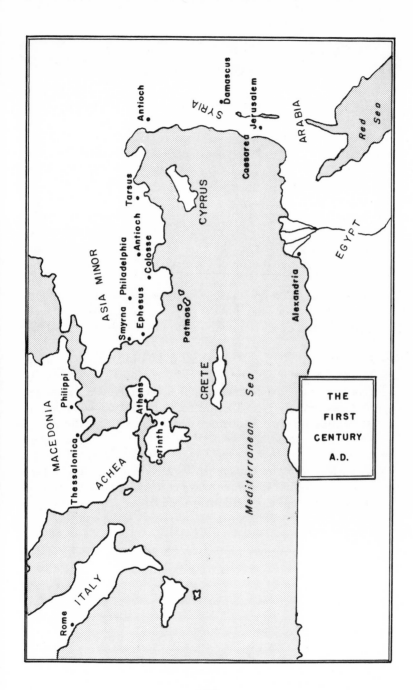

THE
FIRST
CENTURY
A.D.

153

QUESTIONS FOR DISCUSSION

1. What kind of role does God's spirit play in Luke-Acts?

2. What kind of life-style did the earliest Christians in Jerusalem have? Did Luke deem it to be a model for the Christians of his day? In what way can the contemporary Christians reflect such a life-style?

3. Compare the Pentecostal experience described in Acts 1:1–13 with the experience of receiving the spirit by some judges and prophets in the Old Testament. Is such an aberrant spiritual experience required of every Christian?

4. Discuss Paul's conversion experience as described in Acts 9:1–30. Is it necessary for every person to experience such a sudden and drastic conversion in order to be a Christian?

5. According to Acts 11:1–18, how did Peter convince other Jewish Christians of the legitimacy of the Gentile mission? What were the problems and solutions arrived at in the Jerusalem council (Acts 15:1–35)? Do these problems still exist today if one insists strongly on the Jewish heritage?

6. Christianity has been a missionary religion from the beginning. Does it infringe upon others' freedom if you try to convert them? What are some ways of sharing your faith with others? How did early Christians do it?

Chapter Four

THE LETTERS OF PAUL

Of the twenty-seven books of the New Testament, thirteen are ascribed to Paul. However, not all of them seem to have been written by him. Modern scholars generally accept the Pauline authenticity of 1 Thessalonians, Galatians, 1 and 2 Corinthians, Philippians, Philemon, and Romans, but regard the rest either as pseudonymous or spurious. In this chapter, therefore, we will discuss the seven undisputed letters of Paul.

All of these letters were written in order to meet a particular need; they answer questions, instead of giving a series of deliberately systematized presentations of Paul's theology. They were produced and read in turbulent conditions—the young and widespread churches were far from being well organized, both doctrinally and administratively, and were under persecution and facing varied opposition.

Many such letters must have been sent occasionally from Church leaders like Paul to local Christian communities, and some of them were then copied and circulated among various churches, but others have most probably been lost. The extant letters, moreover, cannot have been free from copyists' errors and editorial touches. Sometimes fragments from different letters were combined together, as is most likely the case in 2 Corinthians. Nonetheless, as far as the seven letters by Paul are

155

concerned, from the time of their composition (about twenty to thirty years after Jesus' crucifixion) to this day, they have been preserved rather well over the centuries.

1. THE FIRST LETTER TO THE THESSALONIANS

This letter, in all probability, is the earliest (ca. A.D. 50) of the extant letters of Paul, written for the sake of the Christians of Thessalonica in Macedonia. According to Acts 17:1–9, during his second missionary journey, Paul, accompanied by Silas and Timothy, visited the town. There he was successful in his mission, but the jealousy of other Jews provoked a riot. Paul and Silas, as a result, escaped from there to take refuge in Beroea. This letter seems to bear out this incident: Paul expresses a strong attachment and concern toward the Christian community of Thessalonica and states that he "could bear it no longer" and sent Timothy to encourage them (1 Thess. 3:1–3). Timothy rejoined Paul at Corinth with "the good news of your [their] faith and love" (3:6) and also with some doctrinal questions concerning eschatology, in particular. Paul thus responded with this letter.

The letter may be divided into two sections: the first section (chapters 1–3) narrates Paul's affection and concern for the Thessalonian Christians, and the second section (chapters 4–5) deals with his instruction regarding the expectation of an imminent end of the world. In his discussion of eschatology (4:13–5:11), Paul reassures the believers that they will be resurrected just as Jesus was raised, and that the last day will come suddenly and in an unexpected way—even as "a thief in the night." Such an eschatological teaching points to the fact that this letter reflects an early stage of Christian development when the intensity of apocalyptic eschatology was predominant.

2. THE LETTER TO THE GALATIANS

This is the only one of Paul's letters which was written for more than one church; it is addressed to the Galatians. Who were these Galatians? This has been a vexing question—some scholars name the Christians in north-central Asia Minor inhabited by the Celtic people, while others suggest the south-central region which Paul, according to Acts 13:14–14:28, visited in his first mission, including such towns as Antioch, Iconium, Lystra, and Derbe. The question remains unsolved, but of importance is the fact that there was, from Paul's point of view, a religious matter of grave concern among the Christians there. This matter, serious enough for Paul to call it "a different Gospel" (1:6), prompted him to write this letter. It was perhaps written in A.D. 53 or 54.

The body of this letter (1:6–6:10) consists of an apologetic against Paul's adversaries to whom the Christians in Galatia had shifted their allegiance. These opponents appear to have been the so-called "Judaizers," i.e., Jewish Christians or the Gentile Christians who were deeply attracted to Judaism. They insisted on the absolute necessity of following the Jewish ancestral law, including circumcision, thereby enabling the Gentile Christians to become the genuine people of God. They wanted to regard Christianity as true Judaism, and therefore they felt Paul's teaching of freedom from the law to be a terrible deviation. Circumcision, for example, was for them a tangible and vital sign of the covenant with God, while for Paul it did not constitute a crucial aspect of Christian life. He summarized his argument as follows: "For in Christ Jesus neither circumcision nor uncircumcision is of any avail, but faith working through love" (5:6).

Paul deploys his contentions in this letter in the ensuing three major areas: (1) his credentials as an apostle (chapters 1–2), (2) the interpretation of the law (3:1–5:12), (3) the freedom in the Spirit (5:13–6:18).

(1) Paul's Credentials as an Apostle

In order to effectively convince his readers of the validity of his position, Paul opens his letter by identifying himself: "Paul an apostle—not from men nor through men, but through Jesus Christ and God the Father" (1:1). Undoubtedly, his opponents must have contested his claim to apostleship by restricting the use of the term "apostle" to mean only the twelve disciples. It is true that Paul had never even met the earthly Jesus; worse still, he had been an erstwhile persecutor of the Church! However, Paul's conviction that he was an apostle, appointed by the risen Christ, was never shaken (1:4–12). The basis of his apostolic claim was the direct revelation of Jesus himself. This direct revelation occurred during his experience on the road to Damascus, which is narrated in 1:13–17.

Compared to the accounts of this event in Acts, Paul's mention of it in this passage is brief but theologically lucid. As K. Stendahl rightly explains, this experience of Paul's is not an oft-alleged conversion, but is a call from God to be an apostle.[1] Paul never "converted" from one religion to another (though that is the usual meaning of conversion). In fact, there seems to be undeniable continuity; he firmly believed in the same God before and after his "conversion." But what is quite explicit in Paul's account in the Galatian passage is a new and special calling of God to his mission. This fact can be corroborated by comparing Paul's words with prophetic calls in the Old Testament (compare Gal. 1:15 with Is. 49:1 and Jer. 1:5). It seems clear from this comparison that Paul viewed his apostleship as legitimate as that of the ancient prophets, for it was the same God who called and sent both the prophets and Paul on a divine mission to the people.

(2) Paul's Interpretation of the Law (3:1–5:12)

The radical shift of Paul's mission from that of a persecutor, zealous for the law, to an apostle of the Gospel entails a different concept of the law. Before this shift, Paul had believed that the law was the supreme manifestation of God's will and that it provided the people with the only way of righteous living. But the new revelation of the risen Christ led him to realize that the law itself would cause the people to place their trust in human beings rather than in God.

The law by itself, moreover, would not give the power to conquer the grave reality of sin. What then would the alternative be? Faith was the answer—faith in God as a voluntary act of commitment to the One who had led him to the awareness of freedom. In the state of faith, people could realize that they were set free from all the traditional and conventional rules and ordinances so as to live with joy in accordance with a higher spirituality. This did not mean, in Paul's opinion, that the law had had no significance; on the contrary, Paul asserted, it had served God's purpose as a "custodian until Christ came" (3:24). "But now that faith has come, we are no longer under a custodian, for in Christ Jesus you are all sons of God, through faith" (v. 25). Jesus showed us, Paul insisted against his adversaries, the true significance of faith so that we are no longer in need of observing the law for the sake of the law, which is a spiritual enslavement, just as he himself was once—driven by his zealous obedience to the law—a merciless persecutor.

(3) Freedom in the Spirit

Faith is an action, an action of freedom. But there is always a temptation to misuse freedom, as typified in the Adam and Eve story in Genesis 3. Thus, Paul admonishes in 5:13: "Only do not use your freedom as an opportunity for the flesh, but through love be servants of one another." Paul often uses the word "flesh" in his writings in various ways. He does not mean by it the inferiority or sinfulness of physical beings in general (as found in Greek philosophy), for there is no such physical vs. non-physical dualism in Paul. But it symbolically indicates ungodly desires and action (cf. 5:19–20).

"Spirit" is the antonym of "flesh." God's Spirit generates a genuine love (*agape* in Greek). Paul states, "For the whole law is fulfilled in one word, 'You shall love your neighbor as yourself' " (5:14). Love is the one and only basis for Christian moral life. Love is a dynamism toward union; genuine love creates a morally desirable social structure as well as truly meaningful human relationships. Paul is underscoring this fact, criticizing his opponents who caused a schism among the Christians. By urging all òf them to "walk by the Spirit" rather than to submit to the legal precepts, he is also effectively eliminating the obstacle which Jewish law presents for the

Gentiles. Paul's Letter to the Galatians is thus an epistle of fierce controversy declaring the validity of his Gospel.

3. THE FIRST LETTER TO THE CORINTHIANS

The Roman city of Corinth was a thriving commercial center at the time Paul visited, founded a church, and subsequently carried on correspondence with the Christians there. Matching the city's cosmopolitan character, the church of Corinth consisted of a variety of people: Gentiles and Jews, former and present slaves, and the rich and poor. Paul apparently continued corresponding with the Corinthian Christians after his visit in A.D. 51. (A series of his correspondences with the Corinthians will be discussed in the next section.)

The extant letters of Paul to the Corinthians demonstrate his continuing intimate concern for them. 1 Corinthians was sent in response to the Corinthians' communication, perhaps from Ephesus, a few years after his visit in A.D. 51 (cf. 1:11; 7:1).

In the first half of the letter (1:10–6:20), Paul deals with the matters reported to him, which include the factions within the church (1:10–4:21) and various moral issues (5:1–6:20). One of the major concerns in this letter relates to the fact that there were several factions among the Christian community in Corinth which were competing one with another, each claiming support and allegiance with certain spiritual fathers such as Paul, Peter, Apollos, etc.[2]

Paul appeals to them that "there be no dissensions among you, but [that] you be united in the same mind and the same judgment" (1:10). In order to reinforce his appeal, he points out that such divisiveness stems from human judgment, which often contradicts diametrically God's judgment: "God chose what is foolish in the world to shame the wise; God chose what is weak in the world to shame the strong . . ." (1:27). Human fame, eloquence, wisdom, power, and so on, cannot provide the followers of God with the condition of allegiance. Rather, when and only when they realize the frailty and vanity of these supposed virtues will there be true unity centered in God. Such a recognition comes only from spiritual maturity. Paul explains it by using the analogies of buildings; it is God who nurtures, it is God who builds, and Paul, Apollos, and the others are nothing more than mere workers (3:1–9).

So, "you are God's building," Paul states, "God's temple" in which God's Spirit dwells (3:16). This concept provides Paul with the basis for his moral admonitions in chapters 5–6.[3] Because the human body is God's temple, it is not at one's own disposal, but it should rather be used for right purposes with love and respect. Paul thus declares: "The body is not meant for immorality, but for the Lord, and the Lord for the body" (6:13).

In the second half of the letter (7:1–15:58), Paul attempts to respond to the Corinthian Christians' request for guidance in a number of practical matters.

(1) Concerning Marital and Sexual Problems (7:1–40)

Paul discusses these questions with an intense feeling of the imminent coming of the end of the world as stated in 7:26: "I think that in view of the impending distress it is well for a person to remain as he is." "For the form of this world is passing away" (7:31), so if married, don't dissolve the marriage; if single, stay unmarried (7:8–11).

Though decidedly ascetic, Paul is not "anti-sex." Sex is a part of the activities of the human body, which is God's temple. Any misuse of sex is a defilement of the sanctity of the body. Though not encouraging, Paul is not "anti-marriage." In fact, he applies a marriage analogy to the relationship between Christ (bridegroom) and Christians (bride) in 2 Corinthians 11:2. Furthermore, he declares that "there is neither male nor female; for you are all one in Christ Jesus" (Gal. 3:28). The important point is, according to Paul, "to promote good order and to secure undivided devotion to the Lord" (7:35). As Constance Parvey states, "Paul's theology of equivalence in Christ provided a vehicle for building a new religious and social basis for women-men relationships in the future," despite the fact that the New Testament writers including Paul often betray a male-dominant religious and cultural cast of the first century Jewish society.[4]

(2) Concerning Meat Offered to Idols (8:1–11:1)

Much of the meat available at the markets in Corinth came from pagan temples where it had been offered as sacrificial animals for idols. Some Christians decided to buy it for their use, claiming that idols were not the true God and thus lacked any real existence, while others strictly stayed away from such a practice. This is one example of the difficulties of living in pagan surroundings. Paul theoretically sided with the former, but strongly urged these emancipated liberals to have a warm understanding and concern toward those who were troubled by it. We are free, Paul says, even in the case of eating pagan meat, but he adds that freedom should be used for "God's glory" (10:31).

(3) Concerning Some Regulations of Worship (11:2–34)

The next question Paul deals with concerns their common worship. He believes that it is improper for women to diverge from the traditional custom of worshiping with their heads covered with a veil (11:2–16).

The next item concerning worship is the observance of the Lord's Supper (11:17–34). As we read in Acts 2:46, the early Christians congregated to share a common meal for the sake of fellowship in this one faith. In the Corinthian church, however, the meaning of this communal meal was neglected, and as a result various undesirable developments, such as divisions and frivolities, took place among them. Paul, therefore, instructs them that the meal is a solemn commemoration of the sacrificial death of Jesus rather than simply being a time of fellowship.

In order to substantiate this admonition, he states in 11:23–26 the tradition concerning the Lord's Supper which he claims to have come from Christ himself. This passage (which describes what Jesus said about the bread and wine at the last

Passover meal before his arrest) contains one of the oldest teachings of the early Church. Paul, who had not met the earthly Jesus, learned this teaching when he became a member of the young Christian community.

The bread represents his body, and the wine his blood (i.e., his life), which were offered to establish a "new covenant" (cf. Jeremiah's prophecy of the new covenant in 31:31–33) between God and the people. Every time Christians partake of these elements, the covenantal relationship (i.e., salvation) is remembered anew; it is to be repeated until the second coming of Christ. In fact, the celebration of the Lord's Supper constituted the basis and goal of Christian worship in the ancient Church.

(4) Concerning the Gift of the Spirit (12:1–14:40)

Another disturbing problem of the Christians in Corinth was the prolific practice of speaking in tongues (i.e., unintelligible ecstatic speech). They attributed this gift to God's Spirit and claimed that their ability was a hallmark of faith. Paul never denied the legitimacy of such a religious practice, but he expressed his concern with the divisive tendency it precipitated. In this passage, he insists on the equal significance of the various gifts of the Spirit, not only speaking in tongues but also wisdom, healing, prophecy, and so on. Different people have different God-given capacities and functions. Each member comprises the whole—"the body of Christ"—in his or her own way and condition. Without genuine diversity, there is no genuine unity. But, Paul goes on to urge, "Desire the higher gift. And I will show you a still more excellent way" (12:31). And that is love (*agape*).

1 Corinthians 13 is perhaps one of the most beautiful chapters in the Bible. Some scholars, in view of its lyric quality, have maintained that Paul quoted here a hymn which the ancient Christians actually sang—the hymn of *agape*.

The English word "love" is multivalent. Love as *agape* is not sexual attraction, which requires a release of inner tension (*epithmia* or *libido*), nor simple friendship or sense of soli-

darity which works within the framework of equality or
reciprocity between two parties (*philia*), nor yearning for be-
coming a desirable being by acquiring better objects, which is
vitally conditioned by an object's quality (*eros* in Plato's *Sym-
posium*). Rather, *agape* is a spontaneous, unconditional, and
creative love.[5] It fulfills all other aspects of love. Being such,
it is a genuine love as a dynamism toward union. It transforms
evil to good; it heals wounds. Thus love is vital and ultimate.
Even excellent moral virtues, profound knowledge, uneradica-
ble faith, the ability of speaking in tongues and healing are
nothing without love. "So faith, hope, and love abide, these
three; but the greatest of these is love" (v. 13).

(5) Concerning the Future Resurrection of the Dead (15:1–58)

Paul attempts in this passage to solve the confusion
among the Corinthian Christians as to the resurrection. To
those who deny it, Paul reminds them of the vital significance
of Jesus' resurrection, which generates others' resurrection.
To those who wonder about "what kind of body" after death,
he denies the immortality of the body, which was a popular belief among the ancient Greeks. When we die, we really die;
otherwise there could be no resurrection. But it does not mean
a resurrection of corpses. It rather indicates a transformation
into a "spiritual body." Paul furnishes no explanation about
the "spiritual body" except saying that it is the imperishable
"image of the man of heaven." We may perhaps put it this
way: it is a metamorphosis from a lower to a higher dimension.

In the final chapter, Paul mentions some arrangements
concerning the contribution for the Christians in Jerusalem
and other personal matters. In closing, he uses an Aramaic
prayer, "Maranatha" (Our Lord, come), which originated in
the earliest Christian community in Judaea. And until the
Lord comes, he adds, "My love be with you all in Christ Jesus.
Amen" (v. 24).

4. THE SECOND LETTER TO THE CORINTHIANS

This letter consists of several apparently mutually independent portions of Paul's letters to the Corinthian church. Scholars have attempted to reconstruct a sequence of correspondence between Paul and the Corinthians. In 1 Corinthians 5:9, we read: "I [Paul] wrote to you in my letter not to associate with immoral men." This letter has been lost, and it was followed by 1 Corinthians.

Subsequent to 1 Corinthians, there appears to have been another letter from Paul. According to scholars, it has been preserved in our 2 Corinthians 2:14–7:4, excepting 6:14–7:1. This letter was intended to bring the Corinthians back from some deviant beliefs to the Christian message which Paul had preached. This attempt was unsuccessful, apparently precipitating a quick visit from Paul to Corinth, where he found open antagonism toward him. Facing such a disastrous situation, Paul wrote another emotionally charged polemical letter, which is refered to in 2 Corinthians 2:4: "For I wrote you out of much affliction and anguish of heart and with many tears, not to cause you pain but to let you know the abundant love I have for you." It is, therefore, often called the "tearful letter." A remnant of this letter has been identified with 2 Corinthians 10–13.

The situation of the Corinthian church, however, greatly improved. Upon hearing this good news from Titus, Paul sent to Corinth a letter of reconciliation, which is embedded in 2 Corinthians 1:1–2:13 and 7:5–16. Consequently, according to scholars' analyses, 2 Corinthians comprises several separate fragments of Paul's letters occasioned by various turbulent conditions. An editor collected these fragments into one literary entity, perhaps in the last decade of the first century A.D. To sum up, Paul's letters to Corinth are:

(a) A lost letter (1 Cor. 6:14–7:1)
(b) First Corinthians
(c) 2 Corinthians 2:14–6:13; 7:2–4

(d) The "tearful letter": 2 Cor. 10:1–13:14
(e) 2 Corinthians 1:1–2:13 and 7:5–16

It is unclear who and what exactly created such violent opposition to Paul in the Corinthian church which he had founded. As we have observed, in 1 Corinthians Paul argues against factionalism in this church. But such is not the case in 2 Corinthians, since every part of this writing is addressed to the whole community, and no reference is made to any specific or particular faction. Some scholars believe that some eloquent preachers of the "Judaizers" from Palestine were the principal opponents of Paul. Another scholarly suggestion concerns some Hellenistic Jewish Christian teachers, who, following a Gnostic view, regarded Christ as a "divine man," i.e., an embodiment of the miracle-performing Spirit of God. However, both theories fall short of making a conclusive case.

(1) 2 Corinthians 2:14–6:13; 7:2–4

Paul attempts vehemently to defend as legitimate his authority as an apostle of the Christian Gospel. He then deals with a comparison of the old and new covenants (3:4–18). As opposed to the old Mosaic law, the new relationship established by Christ is truly life-giving, for whereas the former contains codes written in human letters, the latter is a work of the divine Spirit within human hearts. Thus the old covenant is overshadowed by the glory of the new covenant. (This question is discussed more extensively in Romans.)

It is Paul's mission to work for this new covenant and not to preach himself as his adversaries did (4:5). Therefore, "we are afflicted in every way, but not crushed; perplexed, but not driven to despair; persecuted but not forsaken; struck down, but not destroyed," because we are, though simply "earthen vessels," possessing the power of God's Spirit (4:7–9). Here Paul presents again these antitheses: "earthen vessel" (human weakness) and "treasure" (divine power) in 4:7, and "our outer nature" (human frailty) and "our inner nature" (spiritual power in 4:16. These terms correspond to "death" and "life" in 4:10–12, "visible transiency" and "invisible eternity" in 4:18, and "earthly tent we live in" and "a building from God, a house not made with hands, eternal in the heavens" in 5:1.

Such a dichotomous pattern of thinking, however, is quite alien to the Greek philosophical dualism of the body as a prison for the soul. Paul,in fact, explicitly states: "Whether we are at home or away (i.e., physically dead or alive), we make it our aim to please him [Christ]" (5:9). As we have observed in regard to Genesis 3, "death" indicates a severance from God, the source of life, and not simply a departure of the soul from the flesh. Alienation from God is thus "death" caused by sin, and reconciliation with God is salvation (5:18–19). Paul, therefore, strongly urges the Corinthians to accept this reconciliation (5:20) by opening their hearts to him who has been totally sincere and affectionate to them (6:11–13; 7:2–4).

(2) 2 Corinthians 10:1–13:14

This fragment of Paul's "tearful letter" demonstrates his confrontation with his adversaries. Against their criticism that "his bodily presence is weak, and his speech of no account," he defends himself by stressing his strengths. He is proud of his legitimate Hebrew lineage just as his opponents are, and of the fact that he has undergone much persecution and many hardships for the sake of the Christian ministry, including imprisonments, flagellations, stoning, shipwrecks, dangers of various causes, and starvation (11:23–27). He has also had an ineffable mystical experience and received an "abundance of revelations."

However, Paul is well aware of the "foolishness" of blowing his own horn, and he repeatedly apologizes for it (11:1, 16; 12:1, 11, etc.). Consequently, what he really declares in this letter is: "Let him who boasts, boast of the Lord" (10:17), i.e., praise of God for one's goodness rather than self-praise—a Copernican change of value judgment. This enables him to state: "I will all the more gladly boast of my weakness, that the power of Christ may rest upon me ... for when I am weak, then I am strong" (12:9–10).

(3) 2 Corinthians 1:1–2:13; 7:5–16

Titus brought Paul good news: the situation of the Corinthian church had improved to the extent that they accepted Paul. With great joy, Paul gives thanks for the comfort in Christ which overcomes afflictions. Finally, he impresses upon them the importance of reconciliation and forgiveness rather than division, and he states: "I rejoice because I have perfect confidence in you" (7:16).

2 Corinthians consequently reflects the turbulence of the early days in Christian communities which were not yet well organized doctrinally or administratively. There were inner conflicts as well as externally imposed hardships. We must also acknowledge the fact that the early Christians honestly struggled with each and every difficulty.

5. THE LETTER TO THE PHILIPPIANS

Although the integrity of Paul's letter to the Philippians has been disputed, recent scholarship contends that it is composite in nature as in the case of 2 Corinthians. It consists of three separate fragments of different letters by Paul addressed to the Christians in Philippi. Philippi was a Roman colony located in the east of Thessalonica in Macedonia. Paul founded the Christian church there, which was his first congregation in Europe (Acts 16:11–15). There was an amicable relationship between Paul and the Philippian Christians through the years. These fragments of Paul's letters preserved in our Letter to the Philippians reflect this fact.

(1) The First Fragment (4:10–20)

This portion appears to have been written early during Paul's imprisonment to thank the Philippians for a gift which they had sent to encourage him. He then assures them that he has "learned the secret of facing plenty and hunger, abundance and want" because of the constant strengthening of God (4:12–13).

(2) The Second Fragment (1:1–3:1; 4:4–7)

These passages present a further letter of appreciation for the sincere concern of the Philippians. Paul, despite prolonged confinement, is convinced that his imprisonment has "served to advance the Gospel," for "it has become known throughout the whole praetorian guard and to all the rest that my imprisonment is for Christ; and most of the brethren have been made confident in the Lord ... and are much more bold to speak the word of God without fear" (1:12–13). He then encourages his readers to "let your [their] manner of life be worthy of the Gospel of Christ" (1:27) with love and contrite heart as Christ humbled himself to the death on the cross. (Philippians 2:6–11 is a hymn to Christ, possibly of Jewish Christian origin, which Paul inserted here.) Paul's exhortation gains further crescendo: "Rejoice in the Lord always" (4:4).

(3) The Third Fragment (3:2–4:2; 4:8–9)

These verses are a remnant of a letter in which Paul warns the Philippian church against the "Judaizers." We have already observed in other letters Paul's argument against the trend of some early Christians drawn to old Jewish practices such as circumcision. Paul asserts, despite his proud Jewish background, the significance of "righteousness through faith," rather than by observance of the law. Apparently, this letter was occasioned in circumstances quite different from the other two, but it is uncertain whether it was written before or after the imprisonment (ca. A.D. 53–54).

The Letter of Philemon

This short letter of Paul was written during his imprisonment and addressed to a Christian by the name of Philemon. Paul had come into contact with Onesimus, a runaway slave of Philemon, and converted him to Christianity. In this letter, Paul appeals to Philemon, upon sending Onesimus back to his master, to return Onesimus to him again as a helpful fellow worker, and he offers payment for any debt or penalty incurred by the slave. While respecting the conventional law regarding slaves, Paul also requests that Onesimus be accepted "as a beloved brother" (v. 16). This letter was most likely successful. In fact, ancient Church tradition refers to Onesimus, the former slave, as the bishop of Ephesus.

The Letter to the Romans

Romans is the longest and perhaps last letter of Paul in the New Testament. He wrote it in Corinth around A.D. 56, when he was planning to travel to Jerusalem, then to Rome, and eventually even to Spain, envisioning that he would be able to evangelize the western part of the Mediterranean world (15:24, 28). The Roman capital was new to him; he had never visited there and had no jurisdiction over the Christian community there. The letter unfolds the basic aspects of Paul's theology, which he perhaps felt obliged to tender to the new congregation before his visit. Unlike 2 Corinthians, this letter manifests a high integrity, excepting the final chapter which many scholars consider to be a later addition. Paul presented his theological views systematically in this writing; he had never done this in any other letters. Thus Romans is more of a theological essay than an occasional letter like the others which Paul wrote.

The letter opens and closes with greetings and thanksgiving (1:1–15; 15:14–33). The main body can be divided into three sections: (1) the need and significance of salvation (1:16–8:39), (2) the salvation of Jews (chapters 9–11), and (3) moral teaching (12:1–15:13).

(1) The Need and Significance of Salvation (1:16–8:39)

The section opens with a statement of Paul's theological thesis:

> For I am not ashamed of the Gospel: it is the power
> of God for salvation to everyone who has faith, to the
> Jew first and also the Greek. For in it the righteous-
> ness of God is revealed through faith to faith; as it is

written, "He who through faith is righteous shall live" (1:16–17).

The righteousness of God constitutes the center of Paul's discussion. It is, according to Paul, not a static philosophical notion, nor does it have some sort of desirable moral or legal quality, but it is a power of God which brings people to, and preserves them in, a correct and proper relationship with God. Paul's understanding of the word is derived from the Old Testament, where righteousness and salvation are, in fact, sometimes used synonymously (e.g., Is. 51:5). The right relationship between God and people comprises the authentic world. However, human ungodliness and wickedness blemished this true reality (Rom. 1:18). In order to restore the original authentic world, Christ sacrificed himself, which is indeed God's action to reconcile people with himself.

"Reconciliation" indicates an action of restoring a lost harmonious relationship by removing enmity. It thus re-creates oneness; wounds are healed, and severance is overcome. It entails that individuals gain integrity within themselves, that harmony prevails among people, and that God and the world become truly united. The reconciliation means atonement (at-one-ment), a recovery of wholeness. Wholeness is a state of whole-some-ness. Christian salvation intends to achieve this wholeness. (In fact, many modern psychologists concur in stressing the significance of the concept of wholeness or completeness. J. A. Hadfield states: "In religion the craving for completeness and the sense of incompleteness is well marked; indeed, it appears to be the basis of religion."[6] And C. G. Jung defines religion as "the fruit and culmination of the completeness of life."[7])

That which is vitally exigent to the people is to have faith in God's reconciliation. Faith is a voluntary act of accepting such benevolent power of God. The life of faith is the authentic human life. Paul forcefully contends that it is faith which alone leads to the ultimate salvation by God. It is not gained by observing the written law. What the law entails is obligation, while faith hinges upon individual decision-making free will. The latter nurtures a mature autonomous self, emancipated from the heteronomous demands of the former.

To reinforce his discussion, Paul quotes a passage from the Old Testament prophet Habakkuk: "The righteous shall live by his faith" (2:4). It is Paul's ineradicable conviction that God's salvific acts have already been revealed to the Jews, and now through Christ even to the Gentiles, and that God called Paul to spread this message of salvation "to Greeks and to barbarians, both to the wise and to the foolish," i.e., the whole world (v. 14). Paul strives to convince his readers of the significance of his mission by underscoring the contention that it fits into God's plan for the salvation of all humanity.

The first section (chapters 1–8) is devoted to just this crucial point, i.e., that God's gift of salvation has become available through Christ to everyone. In order to illumine further this contention, Paul admits that the Jews are privileged by being entrusted with God's revelation, the Old Testament; however, that which is crucial involves a trustful execution of God's will, rather than a possession of the law or a practice of circumcision. In fact, everyone is "under the power of sin." The law, though holy, only elicits the consciousness of sin and fails to provide sinners with a definitive vehicle for salvation (3:20).

"But now the righteousness of God has been manifested apart from the law, although the law and the prophets bear witness to it, the righteousness of God through faith in Jesus Christ for all who believe" (3:21–22). This passage marks a decisive turning point in Paul's discussion. The ancient Israelite and Jewish religious heritage is important, for it manifests God's concern with the people, and it is also of great significance that it bears witness to the decisive revelation of God's salvation through Christ. But it is through Christ, not the law, that the divine righteousness which vitally transforms the unrighteous to the righteous is manifested. Therefore, only through faith in the divine salvation of Christ can one be reckoned as acceptable to God.

This belief of "righteousness through faith," Paul affirms,

in no way entails overthrowing the law by faith. On the contrary, the law is upheld because of this faith (3:31). In other words, if faith which is available to any person, Jew or Gentile, enables that person to be restored to his or her authentic place in relation to God and to others, then the goal of the law itself is attained. Paul goes on by calling attention to an example from the Old Testament: Abraham, the father of the Jewish people, was reckoned as righteous because of his faith in God's promise (chapter 4).

In chapter 5, the scope of Paul's explanation of God's salvation through Christ expands, from the Jewish nation to mankind in general, by comparing Christ with Adam. It is interesting to note that Paul does not teach a doctrine of inherited original sin in this chapter. Adam represents the whole humanity who died in sin, but, by contrast, Christ's death brought about life by liberating people from sin. Therefore, Paul forcefully urges his readers not to stay in sin, "for the wages of sin is death, but the free gift of God is eternal life in Christ Jesus our Lord" (6:23).

However, keeping in the righteous way of course requires serious struggle on the part of individuals. A conscientious human soul truly resonates with honest confession in 7:19: "For I do not do the good I want, but the evil I do not want [to do] is what I do." However, "thanks to God through Jesus Christ," the people of faith can be rescued from the miserable struggle through the aid of God's Spirit. "For all who are led by the Spirit of God are sons of God ... and if children, then heirs, heirs of God and fellow heirs with Christ, provided we suffer with him in order that we may also be glorified with him" (8:14–17).

(2) Salvation of Jews (9:1–11:36)

In chapters 9–11, Paul expresses his profound concern about the Jewish people. They are the descendants of God's chosen people and the heirs of God's promise of salvation. Besides, Paul himself was a proud Jew. However, to his great dismay, many of his fellow Jews have not been willing to accept the Christian message. He honestly confesses that this fact causes "great sorrow that I myself am accursed and cut off from Christ for the sake of my brethren, my kinsmen by race" (9:3). Has God decided to abandon them entirely? To answer this painful question, Paul attempts to get across several points. First of all, by using the sons of Abraham as an example (9:6–10), he points out that not every physical descendant of Abraham is included in God's plan of salvation. This is so because God has unlimited freedom of discretion, which no human being can question. In fact, Paul continues to say, God has the right and power to choose not only from the Jews but also from the Gentiles. Secondly, Israel who pursued righteousness through the observance of the law failed in fulfilling the law. Instead, the fulfillment of the divine law could be brought about only through faith. As he puts it, "Christ is the end of the law, that everyone who has faith may be justified" (10:4). Ironically, therefore, the Gentiles who were outside of God's original plan of salvation obtained righteousness through faith (9:30–32).

Paul's third point concerns the question: "Has God rejected his people?" His response to this question is an emphatic "no." Here Paul brings forward the old prophetic notion of the righteous remnant: only righteous ones of Israel were chosen to be the heirs of God's grace. As of old, "there is a remnant, chosen by grace" (11:5). However, it is Paul's firm conviction that this "hardening [that] has come upon part of Israel" (i.e., the Jews who do not accept Christ) will continue "until the full number of the Gentiles come in" to salvation. Then "all Israel will be saved" (11:25–26). Despite the obduracy of the people, Jew or Gentile, God will ultimately reconcile everyone to himself. "For from him and through him and to him are all things" (11:36)—that wholeness will be achieved!

(3) Moral Teaching (12:1–15:13)

The final section of the letter consists of moral exhortations: Paul urges his readers to offer themselves as "a living sacrifice . . . which is true spiritual worship" (12:1). By saying this, Paul perhaps contrasts such a spiritual and moral life of divine worship with the Jewish and pagan sacrifices of animals. Spiritual worship demands that the worshipers avoid conformity to worldly things, preserve modesty, keep a genuine love toward one another and live peacefully together. "Do not be overcome by evil, but overcome evil with good" (12:21). After recommending civil obedience (13:1–7), he further assures the readers that love for neighbor fulfills the law. Paul closes his letter with a blessing in the name of "the God of hope" (15:13).

QUESTIONS FOR DISCUSSION

1. What is the basis for Paul's claim of apostleship (cf. Gal. 1:1–24; 2 Cor. 2:14–3:3)? Are contemporary clergy persons called by God in the same way as the ancient Old Testament prophets and New Testament apostles?

2. What was Paul's understanding of the significance of the law? What kind of meaning does the Old Testament law have for us today? Is there a difference in the interpretation of the law by Paul and us?

3. What was the condition in the church of Corinth? What kind of problems did it have? Do the modern churches share some of these problems? If so, what would Paul have to say about the situation?

4. What does Paul mean by "the human body is God's temple"? In what way can this symbolism be applied to some of the moral questions of today concerning human value?

5. Compare Paul's reference to the Lord's Supper (1 Cor. 11:17–34) with the Gospel writers' narratives of the Last Supper (Mt. 26:26–29; Mk. 14:22–25; Lk. 22:14–20). Are there any significant theological differences among them?

6. What is *agape*? Why do the New Testament writers emphasize it so much? Is there an equivalent concept found in the Old Testament? In what way can *agape* be alive among us?

7. What is Paul's teaching of "righteousness through faith"? Is Paul's idea of righteousness the same as the modern concept of justice?

8. Explain how the idea of "wholeness" is related to (a) salvation history, (b) the Church as Christ's body, and (c) the forgiveness of sins.

Chapter Five

THE DEUTERO-PAULINE AND
PASTORAL LETTERS

While 2 Thessalonians, Colossians, Ephesians, 1 and 2 Timothy, and Titus bear Paul's name as the author, many modern scholars are of the opinion that in reality they were pseudonymously written after the death of the apostle. The writers are unknown, but were most likely Paul's disciples who consciously attempted to imitate and identify themselves with their teacher. 2 Thessalonians, Colossians, and Ephesians were composed perhaps in the seventies A.D., whereas 1 and 2 Timothy and Titus (called the Pastoral Letters) were probably written around the turn of the first century A.D.

1. THE SECOND LETTER TO THE THESSALONIANS

Despite an apparent resemblance of words and central topic, 2 Thessalonians betrays a considerable difference from 1 Thessalonians in theological view. In both of these letters, eschatology is the subject matter. But in 1 Thessalonians, the end of this world is imminent; it will come "like a thief in the night." In 2 Thessalonians, however, the end will not come soon, but rather it will visit after certain satanic events have occurred (2:1–12).

> Let no one deceive you in any way; for that day (the day of the Lord) will not come, unless the rebellion comes first, and the man of lawlessness is revealed. . . ." (2:3).

The distinctive eschatological view of 2 Thessalonians is closer to that which the apocalyptic author of Revelation presents, and it indicates intense persecution.

2. THE LETTER TO THE COLOSSIANS

The authenticity of this letter has been a subject of scholarly debate. Some critics insist on its non-Pauline authorship for the following reasons: (1) its literary style, which is not characteristically Pauline, (2) its theological tenor (especially Christology), which differs from that of Paul's undisputed letters, (3) its curious theological proximity to Ephesians, of which Pauline authenticity is highly suspect, (4) its reflection of the Church as a more organized institution than the freer and less organized Church of Paul's time. It seems therefore that either the letter was written or substantially rewritten later by Paul's disciple.

The town of Colossae was located on the Lycus River in the southwestern part of Asia Minor. Paul himself never visited the town, but Epaphras, whom Paul called "our beloved fellow servant" and "a faithful minister of Christ" (Col. 1:7), founded the church there. This Colossian church at that time, however, was influenced by heretical teachings involving cosmic spirits such as angels (2:8). Christ was absorbed into the hierarchical system of these forces which controlled people. Religious practices foreign to the Christian faith, including feast days, visions, asceticism, circumcision, and food laws were given great emphasis (2:16–18). Such a trend seemingly stemmed from some syncretic religious ideas combining Judaism and the pagan religions predominant in that region.

This letter was intended to combat this confused condition of the Colossian community. Therefore the principal contention of this letter pertains to the understanding of Christ. It is emphatically stated in 1:15: "He is the image of the invisible God, the first-born of all creation." (Many scholars are of the opinion that 1:15–20 was originally an early Christian liturgical hymn. Whatever the provenance may be, this section comprises the central message of the whole writing.) Christ, as the decisive revelation of God, precedes everything in this cosmos. "All things were created through him and for him" (v. 16). The words "through" and "for" in this verse indicate that Christ is the unifying center of "all things" (including the spiritual powers in which the Colossians were interested). Thus we read in verse 19: ". . . and through him to reconcile to himself all things, whether on earth or in heaven, making peace by the blood of his cross." Here the Pauline concept of Christ's reconciliation as a restoration of wholeness (which we observed in Romans) finds a more explicit demonstration.

On the basis of such a teaching of the "cosmic Christ," the author repeatedly warns against false teachings and practices (2:8–23). Such "philosophy and empty deceit" stem from nothing but human ideas and are not "according to Christ" who is "the head of all rule and authority." The Christians were to receive not a physical circumcision but "the circumcision of Christ," i.e., a liberation from all these human traditions, teachings, and practices (taboos, ascetic self-abasement, etc.). The author then proceeds to urge the readers to let love and peace prevail among them, for love "binds everything together in perfect harmony" (3:14).

3. THE LETTER TO THE EPHESIANS

The pseudonymity of this letter is even more clearly detected than in Colossians. Its literary style is even less Pauline, and seventy-three of the total of one hundred and fifty-five verses in Ephesians have verbal parallels with Colossians. Another peculiar fact of Ephesians is that there is no hint of the concrete occasion of the writing of this letter, and there is no polemic intention (unlike the other Pauline or deutero-Pauline letters). Moreover, the letter's addressee is uncertain, for in the best ancient manuscripts of this letter the opening address (1:1) lacks a reference to the Ephesians; it says simply: "To the saints who are also faithful in Christ Jesus." It is more likely that this letter was originally intended to be addressed to all Christians rather than to be sent to a particular church. Therefore, modern scholars sometimes call it a "tract" or "encyclical."

The idea of unity constitutes the main theme of the letter, which comprises a doctrinal section (chapters 1–3) and a section of moral exhortations (chapters 4–6). The doctrinal part opens with praise for God and his cosmic plan of salvation. God, according to this author, had designed the salvific program before the universe came to exist, and in "the fullness of time" united all things through Christ. Here the Colossian "cosmic Christology" is reitereated (cf. also 4:8–10). God first revealed his will to the Jews and then to the Gentiles as they received the Gospel and the Holy Spirit.

The readers (who are Gentiles) are reminded of their past situation when they were excluded from that group of people of the chosen people of God, but they are assured also that Christ's death brought about perfect union between the Jews and Gentiles. He "has broken down the dividing wall of hostility" (2:14). This symbolic "dividing wall" seems to refer also to a stone partition which separated the inner court (only for the Jews) from the outer court (for the Gentiles) in the Jerusalem temple. There were signs posted on the wall prohibiting any Gentile from entering the inner court under penalty of death.[1] The author maintains that by virtue of Christ's sacrifice, however, such alienation was removed and true peace proclaimed both to "those who were far off and those who were near," so that they are assembled to form a spiritual temple where there is no dividing wall. And Christ himself is "the chief cornerstone" of this "temple," i.e., the Church.

In the moral exhortations which comprise the second half of the letter, too, the theme of unity plays a key role. The unity of faith and the Church is repeatedly underscored: there is "one Lord, one faith, one baptism, one God and Father of us all" (4:5–6). The Church is compared to a physical body in which every part (member) is joined together properly so as to grow in love (4:16). The same harmony should be kept alive always in each family (5:21–6:9). The moral exhortations of this letter close with an admonition against "the wiles of the devil" (6:11) that are to be avoided by leading a life of moral goodness and incessant prayer.

4. THE PASTORAL LETTERS

Since the eighteenth century, 1 and 2 Timothy and Titus have been grouped together and called "the Pastoral Letters." All three of these letters concern the pastoral ministry, ostensibly written by Paul for the sake of his younger colleagues, Timothy and Titus. The pseudonymity of these letters is now widely recognized. First, their literary style (above all, their vocabulary) is not Pauline. Second, their theological posture is far more conventional when compared to Paul's creative and inspirational theology. The Pastoral Letters' basic concern is to preserve the apostolic teachings. For example, "faith" means obedient acceptance of doctrine (e.g., Titus 1:1; 2:10), rather than the living action of a trusting commitment as Paul had emphasized. Third, as will be observed later, the Church organization reflected in these letters is decidedly more developed and stabilized than that of Paul's time.

Who then was the author(s) of these letters? The answer is beyond our reach, though he was most probably a person of eminent position in the churches founded and/or nurtured by Paul in Asia Minor. The author wrote these letters perhaps in the very early second century A.D. to the leaders of the local churches for the purpose of giving instructions germane to their pastoral problems. Consequently, "Timothy" and "Titus" are also pseudonymous, and not the Timothy and Titus who were companions of Paul.

All three letters share the same basic concern, which can be summarized as: (1) the avoidance of heresy, (2) holding fast to apostolic doctrine, and (3) the pious life. The heresy against which the author is warning appears to be, though not mentioned by name, Gnosticism. We read in 1 Timothy 6:20: "Guard what has been entrusted to you. Avoid godless chatter and contradictions of what is falsely called knowledge (*gnosis* in Greek)."

A stronghold against every kind of heresy is the apostolic doctrine. The author(s) of the Pastoral Letters belonged to the second Christian generation, when the authenticity of the Christian faith was sought in apostolicity. Therefore, the proper form of Christian living safeguards against heresies and involves consistent faithfulness to the apostolic teachings. In 2 Timothy, in particular, the reader is urged to follow Paul who has suffered, is fettered in prison and awaits martyrdom (1:1–13).

The author further admonishes that Church leaders such as the bishops, deacons, and elders should be modest, generous, and self-disciplined men who keep their families so well and proper as to prove their ability to lead the Church (1 Tim. 3; Titus 1:6–9). Advice is also given to treat elder people and widows with love and respect (1 Tim. 5). Mutual peace and obedience to authorities are also recommended. In all, the Pastoral Letters mark a process shifting from the inspirational apostolic period to an era of a more organized and stable Church.

QUESTIONS FOR DISCUSSION

1. There is a difference of view concerning eschatology between 1 and 2 Thessalonians. Why did such a difference come to exist? What is a proper modern interpretation of this conflict?

2. What kind of view concerning Christ is presented in Colossians? Are there similar views presented in the other writings of the New Testament?

3. Explain the symbol of the Church as God's temple, and relate this symbolism to the contemporary Church.

4. How is the emphasis on unity in Ephesians related to the Deuteronomic theological theme of oneness? Has such a theological notion inspired contemporary socio-religious movements?

5. What does "faith" mean in the Pastoral Letters? Compare it with Paul's idea. To which is modern Christians' "faith" closer? Why so?

6. Write a pastoral letter to the modern Church.

Chapter Six

HEBREWS AND THE
CATHOLIC LETTERS

1. THE LETTER TO THE HEBREWS

This writing, despite the title (which is secondary), is not a letter, but a sermon or a theological treatise; its style and content demand that judgment, and it also lacks reference to its addressee, though it ends like a letter (13:18–25).

The Pauline authorship of this book has been claimed traditionally, but doubt of this can be traced even to the time of the Church Fathers. It is now universally recognized that the book manifests a literary style and theological tenets quite distinct from Paul's. The writer demonstrates good Greek literary skill and a profound interest and knowledge about the Old Testament and rabbinical interpretative methods of Scripture. In fact, there are more quotations from the Old Testament in this writing than in any other New Testament book. Consequently, modern scholars generally are of the opinion that the author was a Hellenized Jewish Christian writing on behalf of the Hellenized Jewish Christians.

The date and place of composition of the book are uncertain, but the date cannot be too early, since some passages hint that the author belonged to a second generation Chris-

tian group (2:3; 10:32–34). The fact that the First Letter of
Clement (A.D. 96) contains quotations from Hebrews attests
that our book must have been written before this date. Many
contemporary scholars think that since the author strongly
urges the readers to patiently remain firm in the faith (10:32–
39; 12:1–17), the writer and the readers were under serious
persecution, perhaps under the Roman emperor Domitian
(A.D. 81–96). Hebrews is thus considered to have been written
to encourage Christians during that time of hardship. Scholars also suggest that the place of composition was Rome, since
Clement, the bishop of Rome, quoted Hebrews within what
could only have been a few years of its writing.

The content of Hebrews is as follows:

(1) The superiority of Jesus (1:1–4:13)
(2) Jesus as high priest (4:14–10:39)
(3) Faith and discipline (11:1–13:17)
(4) Postscript and benediction (13:18–25)

(1) The Superiority of Jesus (1:1–4:13)

The author opens his writing with the proclamation that
Jesus is the Son of God, who is both heir and agent of creation
and the Savior of humankind (1:1–4). To expand on this decisive significance of Jesus, the author discusses the superiority
of Jesus both in a superhuman and human dimension.

First, in the superhuman dimension, Jesus is superior to
angels (1:5–2:18) because (a) he is the Son of God, (b) he is en-
throned over the universe, while angels are simply servants of
God, yet (c) God made him temporarily lower than angels in
order to save mankind through his suffering and death, and
then glorified him higher than angels.

The author proceeds to the human dimension by explaining Jesus' superiority over Moses (3:1–4:13). Moses was a faithful servant of Israel, but Jesus is "over" God's people,
including Moses. Israel, under the leadership of Moses, wan-
dered in the wilderness for forty years because of their sin. For
this reason, too, Moses was not able to enter "rest" (the promised land). The author connects this "rest," by using the rab-

binical interpretative method of the day, with the sabbath of God's creation (Gen. 2:2–3), and claims that God ordained the "rest" at the time of creation. But the eternal place of "rest" is now available through Jesus for believers.

(2)   Jesus as High Priest (4:14–10:39)

Biblical authors saw in Jesus the fulfillment of what the Old Testament had foreshadowed: Jesus was viewed variously as the Davidic Messiah, the eschatological prophet, the Wisdom, the suffering servant of God. The author of Hebrews perceived in a similar vein that the priestly tradition of Israel was fulfilled by Jesus; that is, Jesus was the true high priest at the eschatological time.

In a major part of Hebrews (4:14–10:39), the author contends that Jesus was the high priest after the order of Melchizedek. In other words, Melchizedek constitutes the prototype of Jesus. Melchizedek, mentioned in Genesis 14, is the priest-king who blessed Abraham, and Abraham paid a tithe to him. The author capitalizes on this story to draw out the conclusion that the priesthood of Melchizedek is superior to the Jewish priesthood, an offshoot of Abraham. Therefore, according to the author, Jesus is superior to the Jewish priests.

Our author further explains the meaning of Jesus' priesthood. The most important task of a high priest in Israel was to offer sacrifice to God on behalf of the people. Jesus did exactly that through his death on the cross; he offered himself as a sacrificial victim for the sake not only of Jews but of everyone (9:28). As prescribed in the law, sacrificial animals were supposed to be without blemish; Jesus was sinless—the perfect and unique sacrifice.

Moreover, this self-sacrifice of Jesus occurred once and for all, thereby making the traditional practice of annual sacrifice by the Jewish high priest no longer necessary. The unique priestly function of Jesus through self-sacrifice is thus final and decisive. His high priesthood does not depend on physical descent or legal provision, both of which are found to be ineffective, but it is predicated upon his own perfection. It thus can exercise its eternal efficacy. The author of Hebrews attempts to bolster this contention by quoting Jeremiah's prophecy of the new covenant; Jesus became the mediator of this new covenant, thereby reckoning the old covenant obsolete (chapter 8).

The superiority of Jesus' priesthood also implies the superiority of his sanctuary. As the traditional priesthood and sacrificial rites of the Jews become inadequate shadows of the spiritual meaning of Jesus' priesthood, the earthly, human-made sanctuary as well is only a "copy and shadow" of the true heavenly sanctuary. Jesus, after his sacrificial death, entered the holy of holies of this eternal sanctuary, thereby enabling people access to God's presence (10:19–20).

(3)   Faith and Discipline (11:1–13:7)

Thus, according to our author, the old Jewish sacrificial rite is now obsolete, and that which is in order is a firm belief in God on the basis of Christ's redemption. In the last major section (11:1–13:7), the author, therefore, urges his readers to keep a steady faith. In excellent rhetoric, he lists witnesses to faith in the Old Testament, including Abel, Enoch, Noah, the patriarchs, Moses, and others, all of whom trusted and kept a hope in God's promise despite various difficulties. But none of them received the promise while they were alive, since God's promise was manifested later in Christ. Therefore, the author exhorts: "Let us run with perseverance the race that is set before us, looking to Jesus the pioneer and perfecter of our faith, who for the joy that was set before him endured the cross, despising the shame, and is seated at the right hand of the throne of God" (12:1–2).

2.   THE CATHOLIC LETTERS

The seven letters of the New Testament, including James, 1 and 2 Peter, 1, 2, and 3 John, and Jude, are traditionally called the Catholic Letters. The word catholic means "general," i.e., these letters (excepting 3 John) are addressed to the

Church in general as distinct from those sent to particular churches or individuals as was true of Paul's letters. They are intended to give guidance to Christians in their everyday life under both major and minor harassments and persecution. Excepting 1 Peter and 1 John, the remaining five were not widely accepted as canonical by the Church until the fourth century A.D.

1. The Letter of James

Although it is stated in the opening: "James, a servant of God and of the Lord Jesus Christ, to the twelve tribes in the dispersion: Greeting," this writing does not read like a letter; it rather consists of moral exhortations. The identity of this "James" is uncertain; it proves abortive to equate him with any James known in the New Testament. It seems quite possible that the author was a Jewish Christian teacher who bore this name. The addressee, "the twelve tribes in the dispersion," seems to indicate metaphorically Christians scattered throughout the world. The place of composition eludes us. The date of composition might be toward the end of the first century A.D.

Since this writing, reflecting the Old Testament wisdom sayings, consists of loosely connected moral maxims, its structure cannot be clearly observed. The author exhorts the readers to persevere in faith and to eradicate greed, anger, and prejudice against the poor. Faith without works through love is meaningless, for faith is completed by works (2:14–26). Likewise, words without action are not only unwarranted but even dangerous. As against earthly and devilish wisdom from which comes bitter jealousy and selfish ambition, "the wisdom from above is first pure, then peaceful, gentle, open to reason, full of mercy and good fruits, without uncertainty or insincerity" (3:17).

Inasmuch as the author repeatedly underscores the importance of good works even to the extent of stating that "a man is justified by works and not by faith alone" (2:24), interpreters often consider this writing to be a polemic against the

Pauline assertion of "righteousness through faith" (i.e., a person can be reckoned righteous by God through faith alone). Such an interpretation of James is unwarranted, however. Paul never denies the importance of good works, and what he preaches is "faith working through love" (Gal. 5:6). The author of James agrees with Paul perfectly on this crucial point. He therefore stands in the same vein of Christianity as Paul and represents a Christian piety of a period slightly later than Paul's day.

2. The First Letter of Peter

Although this letter has been ascribed since the second century A.D. to Peter, a disciple of Jesus, it is pseudonymous, because (a) its refined Greek composition could not have been produced by an Aramaic-speaking fisherman of Galilee, (b) there is no personal recollection of Jesus, (c) it presupposes the Pauline theology (e.g., the righteousness based on atonement through Jesus' death stated in 2:24). The letter, addressed to dispersed Christians in Asia Minor (1:1), was written perhaps in Rome ("Babylon" in 5:13 is a cipher for Rome), probably during the persecution under the Roman emperor Trajan (A.D. 98–117).

The content of the letter may be divided into three sections.

(1)   In 1:3–2:10, the author praises God for Christ's resurrection which has given hope of a future salvation. He further admonishes the readers to hold fast to this hope and to live upright lives with mutual love, thereby belonging to the spiritual temple of Christ.

(2)   The second section (2:11–4:11) comprises hortatory warnings concerning civil obedience, compliance, modesty, and understanding in household matters, and preparedness and perseverance against persecution.

(3)   In the closing section (4:12–5:14), the author advises the readers to take hardships not with shame and distress but rather with joy as they participate in Christ's suffering, which brings about God's salvation. He also urges the Church elders

to a humble and conscientious ministry. This letter as a whole reveals a remarkable spirit of persistent love in the face of persecution.

3.   The Letters of John

Since the third century A.D., the Christian Church has attributed these three brief letters to John, a disciple, who was also believed to have written the Fourth Gospel. True, there are noticeable similarities between the Gospel and these letters: they share much common terminology and theological thought. The most striking example of this is their characteristic use of dualistic patterns such as light vs. darkness, life vs. death, truth vs. falsehood, love vs. hate, and so on. However, there are undismissable differences as well. For example, the letters betray no interest in the "realized eschatology" which is of vital significance in the Gospel. 1 John's reference to the "antichrist" is not attested to in the Gospel. Moreover, it is stated that 2 and 3 John were written by the "elder" rather than the apostle (2 Jn. 1:1; 3 Jn. 1:1). Consequently, modern scholars generally hold the view that the elder John who they suppose wrote all three of these letters belonged to the "Johannine community."

These letters of John the Elder were written perhaps in the very early second century A.D. 1 John lacks an addressee, and it reads like a homily rather than a letter. 2 John is addressed to "the elect lady and her children," which probably symbolizes a church. 3 John is rather a personal letter to "Gaius," accusing a certain Diotrephes who exercises power over fellow Christians.

All three writings are intended to safeguard the post-apostolic Church against heresies and to further nurture its unity in love. The heresy with which the author shows special concern is the "antichrist" who "will not acknowledge the coming of Jesus Christ in the flesh" (2 Jn. 7)—the heresy of "docetism" (from Greek *dokein,* "to seem"). Docetism is a teaching which stemmed from Gnosticism. It professes that Jesus was simply human, but the heavenly Christ descended on Jesus at his baptism and the Christ left Jesus before the crucifixion.

Therefore, the Christ just "seemed" to suffer. John the Elder violently denounces such teaching by stating the following: "No one who denies the Son has the Father. He who confesses the Son has the Father also" (1 Jn. 2:23). The parlance of this statement suggests a step toward the creedal confession which Church councils officially declared more than two hundred years later.

The very basic message of the Elder's letters does not really concern his denunciation of docetism, but it reposes in the teaching of love. He repeatedly summons the readers to abide in love (*agape*) which God has manifested through Jesus Christ. In 1 John 4:8, we read the clearest statement about love in the whole Bible: "God is love." *Agape* is genuine love that is willing to sacrifice itself for others in order to bring about true union. The Elder urges: "By this we know love, that [Christ] laid down his life for us; and we ought to lay down our lives for the brethren" (3:16).

4. The Letter of Jude

This very brief letter, though ascribed to "Jude, the brother of James," is pseudonymous, and its author and place of composition are unknown. It was perhaps written in the early second century A.D. and represents one of the later writings of the New Testament. The aim of the letter is to combat existing heresies, though the nature of the dissident views is unclear. The author warns those who desert the traditional Christian faith that they will be judged by God.

5. The Second Letter of Peter

Like the First Letter, this one also bears Peter's name, but it is pseudonymous. The author must be other than the writer of the First Letter, for the Second Letter characteristically uses some Hellenistic concepts (e.g., "partakers of divine nature" in 1:4), and also because of the fact that it reproduces most of the Letter of Jude. Thus many scholars date this letter at approximately A.D. 125, and some even as late as A.D. 150. This is the latest composition of all the New Testament books.

The major issue in the letter concerns an explanation of

the delay of the end of the world. The author advises patience, for "with the Lord one day is as a thousand years, and a thousand years as one day," and because God "is forbearing toward you, not wishing that any should perish, but that all should reach repentance" (3:8–9). This letter reflects the rise of the normative Church as an institution with the authority to refute dissidents and heresies by re-evaluating transmitted Christian traditions.

QUESTIONS FOR DISCUSSION

1. How does the author of Hebrews use the Old Testament? Is it an effective method for getting across his contentions? Does it do justice to the Old Testament itself? Can we use similar ways of interpreting the Old Testament?

2. In what sense, according to Hebrews, is Jesus Christ the true high priest?

3. What is the relationship between "good works" and "faith" in James? Why was this issue especially significant at his time? What about its significance for our situation?

4. What is docetism? Is there any modern version of "docetic Christianity"?

5. How does "God is love" differ from "love is God"?

6. In what way can we follow the teaching of John the Elder that we lay down our lives for our brethren?

Chapter Seven

REVELATION

This last book of the Bible is the only thoroughly apocalyptic writing in the New Testament. The unity and origin of this book has been a subject of scholarly debate. Some scholars held that it was originally a Jewish writing to which minor corrections and insertions (i.e., chapters 1–3; 22:16a, 20b, 21) were added by some Christian editors. The fact that the book repeats images, symbols, and ideas has led other scholars to assume the book's composite nature. However, recent scholarly opinions, recognizing that this repetition was a feature characteristic of apocalyptic literature, increasingly underscore its integrity as well as its Christian authenticity.

The opening verses state that the book records the revelation which God disclosed to the prophet John concerning "what must soon take place." This John must not be John, the disciple of Jesus, because, for example, the author does not include himself in his reference to the disciples (18:20; 21:14). His style and theological perspective are different from that of the writer of the Fourth Gospel. Moreover, he was a seer of visions. However, he might very well have belonged to that "Johannine community." He and his audience were under terrible persecution which apparently the Roman emperor Domitian inflicted upon Christians around A.D. 95.

As Roman history states, Domitian claimed divine parentage and demanded, toward the end of his life, that every subject of the empire give him the devotion of loyalty and worship due to that status. This demand of emperor-worship imposed particularly upon Christians presented a serious challenge to their faith in God. Spiritual loyalty was at stake: Who was the true Lord, God or the emperor? Many of them remained loyal to God, and some suffered martyrdom. Our apocalyptist, John, was seemingly one of those who was banished; he saw visions and wrote this book in exile on the isle of Patmos in the Aegean Sea.

To Domitian, the Christians simply seemed to be a subversive group that should be eradicated. However, the apocalyptist John perceived that there was not fundamentally a political conflict between the Church and the state but a strife between God and evil (satanic power) in a cosmic dimension. The question was, therefore, far more serious than could be solved by some political maneuver. It rather involved the whole value system of human beings, the meaning of their existence, the direction of history, and cosmic order. Such a way of viewing reality constituted a typical apocalyptic perception; it presented a transcendent viewpoint, and not just some kind of extravaganza.

True, the Book of Revelation contains various strange, sometimes bewildering images and highly enigmatic words and statements, many of which are of ancient mythological origin. They have often effected a number of fantastic interpretations throughout generations. Even of late, there are sundry attempts to apply them to actual historical events of the present age (e.g., the beast of 13:11–18 is alleged to be Hitler). Such attempts are vain distortions. The book should be construed in its own situation: the Domitian persecution. Its principal aim is to encourage the Christians to persevere in keeping their genuine faith with the ardent hope for the imminent coming of the end of this world.

To be sure, apocalyptic visions are not products of a revengeful neurotic mind affected by a hostile environment, but they are an extraordinary eruption of a genuine and relentless soul which seeks justice and ultimate retribution from God's hand at a time of grave crisis. The apocalyptist does not consign himself simply to aberrant fantasy, but stands firmly upon the conviction that God is the true and ultimate Lord of history. And thus his message is clear: hope in the divine horizon.

1. SEVEN LETTERS

The content of this book can be divided into three major parts in addition to the prologue (1:1–8) and the epilogue (22:6–21). The first major section comprises the seven letters to the churches in Asia Minor (1:9–3:22). Each letter contains a message to the seven churches of that region written with a similar literary structure, admonishing each of these Christian communities. The apocalyptist is evidently well acquainted with their many problems, including misguidance by false apostles and a prophetess, apostasy, heresy, conflict with Jews, apathetic and dead spiritual conditions, and so on. Yet, some churches are praised for their faithfulness to Christ. Each of these letters closes with a promise of final victory—blissful eternal life—for those who remain loyal in the faith. The letters are addressed to the churches of seven different localities in Asia Minor, but they are, in reality, meant for all Christians, for the number seven symbolizes completeness.

2. VISIONS

In the second major section (5:1–22:5), seven groups of visions portray things to come. The first is the vision of a scroll with seven seals, which can be opened only by the sacrificial lamb, Jesus (5:1–8:1). As the first four are unsealed, war, strife, famine, and death take place. At the loosening of the fifth seal, an announcement is made that in the fullness of time the martyrs will have vengeance, and a violent shaking of the cosmos follows the undoing of the sixth seal. Then comes a visionary scene of a great multitude of white-robed (i.e., atoned) martyrs with the mark of God's ownership on their foreheads (chapter 7). With the breaking of the seventh seal silence falls on the heavens so that the martyrs' prayers can be heard by God. This silence is broken by thunder and earthquakes, which gives seven angels the cue to blow their trumpets in turn.

The vision of the seven trumpets constitutes the second vision of the apocalyptist (8:2–11:19). As the trumpets sound, devastating catastrophes are inflicted upon the earth by fire, satanic locusts, and destruction-bearing troops. As a result, persons lacking the mark of God undergo great suffering; even though they seek death, "death flies from them." The sound of the seventh trumpet initiates the third series of visions concerning the dragon's kingdom (12:1–18).

This vision begins with the appearance of a woman, who, after painful birth pangs, gives birth to a male child. She symbolically represents the people of God, and the child is the Messiah who is to rule the world. But there is a fearful adversary: the dragon which is the epitome of the evil forces. The vision then is of the angels' war against the dragon in heaven. The dragon is defeated and cast down to the earth, but it now goes after the woman.

The fourth vision concerns the beasts upon whom the dragon confers his power (13:1–18). The whole of the inhabitants are afraid and worship these blasphemous powers. This is a reference to Roman emperor-worship. The first beast seemingly symbolizes the empire itself, and the second evidently the emperor Nero who initiated persecution of the Christians. He is referred to cryptically by the number 666, and Neron Caesar spelled in Hebrew has that numerical value. As scholars suggest, however, it indicates not only Nero alone but other emperors as well (above all Domitian) who are "revived" Neros.

The next series of visions (chapter 14) presents Christ as a lamb, with angels urging steadfast faithfulness to Christ, and also their acts of judgment of the worshipers of the beast. The fifth major series of visions portrays seven plagues of judgment (symbolized by the pouring of the seven bowls of God's wrath) by the seven angels (15:1–16:21). This series stands parallel to the plagues of the seven seals and the seven trumpets, but it marks a climax of God's wrath. This series is followed by the visions of the fall of Babylon (a code name for Rome), which is personified as a whore (17:1–19:10). She, Rome, attempts to seduce the world into worshiping a false god, the Roman emperor, with great wealth and beauty, but instead she falls with fire. The catastrophic destruction of Babylon is contrasted with the hosts of angels praising God—the Hallelujah chorus (19:1–10).

The seventh and final series of visions are recorded in 19:11–22:5. They describe the final defeat of the "beast" and his hosts by Christ and the angels. The dragon, the symbol of evil (Satan), is chained, and the martyrs are resurrected to join in the Messiah's rule for a thousand years. (Millenarianism—the belief in an intermediary period of a messianic reign on earth before the last judgment—was an idea rather widely held among early Church Fathers, though it subsequently subsided. A similar idea existed among the Jews and the Samaritans in the pre-Christian period.)

After this period, Satan is let loose and attacks the pious ones in the holy city, but he is overpowered and thrown into eternal fire. Then all the dead are resurrected and judged according to their deeds. The final vision presents a new heaven and earth; no longer does the old heaven and earth exist. The new Jerusalem descends from heaven, thereby uniting heaven and earth. It is the center of the new world of a new dimension, as it is symbolically called "the bride of Christ." In this new world, "neither shall there be mourning nor crying nor pain anymore," for "the dwelling of God is with men" (21:3–4).

Thus ends the Book of Revelation, and the whole Bible. The Bible opens with the great creativity of God (Gen. 1) and closes with the grand re-creation of God's world. It emphatically affirms the purposefulness of history, and confesses God as the source of meaning and hope for the world.

QUESTIONS FOR DISCUSSION

1. What was the occasion for the writing of the Book of Revelation? In a situation like that of the apocalyptist John, what would you do—abandon your faith, or quietly and patiently wait for God's action, or participate in actions against the oppressors, or what? What is John's advice?

2. What are apocalyptic visions? Are they a legitimate religious phenomenon? Can modern people experience them?

3. In Revelation what do the numbers symbolize? Why is this kind of symbolism used? Do modern people use such cryptic literary devices? If so, give some examples.

4. How is Christ depicted in Revelation? Are there any significant differences among Revelation, the Gospels, and Paul's letters in Christ's image?

5. Who is the "bride of Christ"? What qualifies him/her/them to be the "bride"? What is the Old Testament background for this metaphor? In what sense could modern persons also be the "bride"?

6. Do you believe in the end of the world? Give reasons.

Appendix

THE BIBLE AND LITURGY[1]

The Bible was born in, nurtured by, and preserved in worshiping communities. As we have observed again and again, all the biblical writers shared one ultimate goal—the praise of a God who cared for his people with steadfast love and who would guide history toward its fulfillment. Divine worship, in this sense, was the "matrix" of the Bible. Consequently, there is a vital relationship between the Bible and worship. This fact can be attested to from evidence found not only in biblical times but also in the ensuing centuries of Jewish and Christian history.

1. ISRAELITE AND JEWISH WORSHIP

In the Old Testament period, the law was read in the temple, and the priests were its custodians. In many instances, the prophetic words were derived from a cultic background. The psalms were composed, compiled, and actually sung in a liturgical context. During the post-exilic period, divine worship at the synagogues comprised the reading of portions from the Scripture (the Old Testament), expositions thereof, and prayers. The Scripture readings consisted of two lessons. The first was from the Torah, and was divided into one hundred and fifty sections, each of which was read once a week in a triennial cycle. (This is called the Palestinian cycle, while the annual cycle is termed the Babylonian cycle.) The second lesson, taken from the prophetical writings, concluded the Scripture readings. Thus lectionaries were used in the synagogue. The psalms, whose number matched that of the sections of the Torah, were also recited during the worship service.

Such worship held in the synagogue can, therefore, be called the "liturgy of the word" compared to the temple liturgy which centered around sacrificial rites. A distinctive example of the liturgy of the word is found among the Essene community at Qumran who separated themselves from the Jerusalem temple by opposing other major sects such as the Sadducees and the Pharisees. They dedicated themselves day and night to scriptural study, which they deemed as a substitute for the sacrifices at the temple.

2. CHRISTIAN WORSHIP

Early Christians followed the Jewish heritage of divine worship. Jesus himself, in fact, participated in synagogue worship by reading Scripture and preaching. We read in chapter four of Luke's Gospel that Jesus went to the synagogue in Nazareth "as his custom was on the sabbath day" (v. 16). There "he stood up to read; and there was given to him the book of the prophet Isaiah" (v. 17). Here, true to the order of the Jewish worship service, the participants were taking turns reading a given portion of the Scripture. The Torah section had been read, and the assigned reading from the prophets was yet to come. This reading was from Isaiah 61:1-2 and 58:6, which Jesus read (vv. 18–19). Then he explained the passages which he had just read. All of this process was customary during the synagogue service.

Not only Jesus, but also the apostles attended worship in synagogues at various places. Acts 13:14–16 records the same procedure of worship which Paul and Barnabas followed in Antioch on a sabbath day. "After the reading of the law and the prophets, the rulers (i.e., officers) of the synagogue sent to them, saying, 'Brethern, if you have any word of exhortation for the people, say it.' So Paul stood up and motioning with his hand said. . . ." (vv. 15–16).

Some Semitic words which were preserved in the Greek New Testament, such as *Amen, Hallelujah,* and *Hosanna,* came directly from Jewish liturgy.

However, there was one crucial difference between Jewish and Christian worship, for the latter was clearly focused on God's redemption *through Jesus Christ.* Consequently, Scripture (the Old Testament) was read and interpreted by Christians from a decidedly Christological point of view, and the eucharistic celebration, the heart of Christian worship, replaced the Jewish sacrificial rite at the temple.

Also, Christian writings were read alongside the Old Testament during the worship service of the Christian communities at various locales. While the Torah lesson occupied the most important place in the synagogue, readings of Gospel passages, apostolic writings, and the prophets were regarded as a vital part of the church service. As for the psalter, its recitation (usually done antiphonally) continued to play a significant role in Christian worship as in the Jewish liturgy. Early Christians also possessed lectionaries which are patterned after Jewish ones. Sermons were delivered by bishops to explain the biblical passages with added exhortations. Liturgical prayers bore distinctive biblical stamps.

According to Gregory Dix, synax (non-eucharistic worship) was conducted in the following order.[2]

1. Opening greeting by the officiant and reply by the church
2. Lesson
3. Psalmody
4. Lesson (or lessons, separated by psalmody)
5. Sermon
6. Dismissal of those who did not belong to the church
7. Prayers
8. Dismissal of the church

St. Justin Martyr (ca. 100–ca. 165) and St. Hippolytus (ca. 170–ca. 236) left us with some reference to worship practices of their time, which seem to indicate that such a worship service as the one Dix has reconstructed was commonly held and was sometimes followed by the Eucharist or baptism or confirmation. Although the scarcity of information prevents us from gaining a clear-cut picture of the early Christian liturgies, it is quite evident that the Bible played an essential role. Christianity inherited the Jewish "liturgy of the word" (Scripture reading, preaching, psalmody, and public prayer) and molded it into a genuinely Christian celebration of the word of God.

Reading of the Bible was done extensively during daily worship, in particular. Such reading had its parallel and origin in the Jewish custom of morning and evening hours of prayer (which corresponded to the morning and evening sacrificial rites at the temple). We read in Acts that the earliest Christians observed periods of devotion at fixed times (3:1; 10:30, etc.), and the Church Fathers Tertullian (ca. 160–ca. 220) and Origen (ca. 185–ca. 254) mention three periods of the Office.

As monasticism developed, the Liturgy of the Hours was greatly enhanced by monks; following regular schedules, they devoted much time to intensively reading the Bible and patristic homilies. The rule of St. Benedict (sixth century) which was generally accepted by the Western Christian world had two types of Office reading: long lessons at Matins (midnight) and short ones at the other Hours (Lauds, first daylight; Prime, sunrise; Terce, midmorning; Sext, noon; None, midafternoon; Vespers, sunset; Compline, before retiring), thereby reciting the entire psalter (the basis of worship) weekly and also covering the whole Bible within a year.

Such an intensive devotional practice of the daily Office was beyond the concern of the by-and-large illiterate masses of the medieval age. Moreover, around and after the tenth century, the Mass also became the preserve only of the clergy. That is to say, both the Office and the Mass were offered by the clergy on behalf of the laity without the latter really participating in them. The Vulgate, the Latin Bible in which the

Roman Catholic Church placed central importance, was not accessible to the laity. (By the tenth century when the Roman rite was adopted throughout Western Europe, only a very small minority of people—almost exclusively members of the clergy—understood Latin.) As a result, the laity became extremely passive; they were simply the pious spectators of the Mass.

3. REFORMATION

As George Devine says, "liturgical renewal would probably have taken place around the time of the Reformation, had it not been for the turbulent atmosphere of the Reformation itself."[3] In the sixteenth century, Martin Luther, John Calvin, and other Reformers began to insist that every person, including laity as well as clergy, should be involved actively in worship. This assertion was quickened by the Reformers' vigorous opposition to what they considered to be the clerical monopoly of worship and the Bible.

In order to enable and encourage even the common people of his country to approach the Bible easily, Luther translated the entire Bible from its original languages into the German which was in daily use in his society. By using this translation, the worship was conducted in the vernacular of the people.

Calvin went even further, claiming to re-establish the worship of the early Church. His intention led him and other Protestants to decide that only baptism and the Holy Communion were sacraments, with the Council of Trent (1545–1563) defining seven sacraments (this number had begun to appear in Roman Catholic teaching in the eleventh century). While underscoring a strictly biblical worship, depending upon the varying conditions of the different countries and provinces, Calvin allowed variety in liturgical practices.

The heart of the Reformers' worship reposed in the proclamation of the divine word. Therefore, not only scriptural readings but also the exposition of the word through preaching occupied the central portion of their worship service. This did not lead them to put the Eucharist in a secondary place, however. Calvin, for example, urged that Holy Communion should be celebrated regularly every Sunday, as against the Roman Catholic practices of his day in which the faithful received the bread and wine once a year during the Lenten-Easter season. Thus the basic structure of the Calvinist church worship was threefold:

1. An introductory praise and confession
2. The service of the word
3. The service of the table

This structure jettisoned much of the traditionally cherished liturgical forms and symbols, though the Lutheran and Anglican churches were more conservative in this respect.

Both Luther and Calvin put great emphasis on the psalmody; the congregation was urged to sing the psalms during the services. Luther, in the spirit of a singing church, even wrote some thirty-seven hymns. Again the idea claimed here was an emphasis on every member's personal and active involvement in a biblical worship.

4. THE SECOND VATICAN COUNCIL

The Second Vatican Council (1962–1965) has exercised revolutionary effects truly as drastic as the Reformation but without such shattering results. Modern Catholicism dawned at this Council.

Biblical Renewal

We may cite first the biblical renewal brought about by the Council. The Council declared that "easy access to Sacred Scripture should be provided for all the Christian faithful" (*Dogmatic Constitution on Divine Revelation,* n. 22).[4] To achieve this goal, it encouraged the translation of the Bible from its original texts into various modern languages. Biblical studies are considered to be "the soul of sacred theology," since "sacred theology rests on the written word of God, together with sacred tradition, as its primary and perpetual foundation," and "by scrutinizing in the light of faith all truth stored up in the mystery of Christ, theology is most powerful and constantly rejuvenated by that word" (n. 24).

Liturgical Renewal

Such a pronounced emphasis on the Bible accompanied another important aspect of the Council's reforming endeavor—the liturgical renewal. The Council affirmed solemnly Christ's presence in the Church's liturgies as well as in the word. "He is present in his word, since it is he himself who speaks when the holy Scriptures are read in the church. He is present, finally, when the church prays and sings. . . ." (*Constitution on the Sacred Liturgy,* n. 7).

In such a liturgy, a vital part of Christian life, "all the faithful" must be led to a "full, conscious, and active participation" (n. 14). The liturgy is to be celebrated in the vernacular (n. 36), and common prayers are to be said by the congregation (n. 53). It is strongly recommended that reception of Holy Communion by all present be seen as the prayer form of celebration. In contrast to the old hierarchical liturgy which was the preserve of the clergy, the contemporary Catholic liturgy is the *communal* worship of all believers. The renewal movements concerning the Bible and the liturgy are vitally united with each other.

Biblical Liturgy

The Council underscored the central significance of the Bible in liturgy.

Sacred Scripture is of paramount importance in the celebration of the liturgy. For it is from Scripture that lessons are read and explained in the homily and psalms are sung; the prayers, collects, and liturgical songs are scriptural in their inspiration, and it is from Scripture that actions and signs derive their meaning (n. 24).

It is also stated in article 51:

> The treasures of the Bible are to be opened up more
> lavishly, so that richer fare may be provided for the
> faithful at the table of God's word. In this way a more
> representative portion of the holy Scriptures will be
> read to the people over a set cycle of years.

The Mass consists of the two major sections: the liturgy of
the word and the Eucharist. As the Council enunciates, these
two form "but one single act of worship" (n. 56). Compared to
the liturgical practice of the pre-Second Vatican Council
which contained two readings each Sunday which were repeated annually, the revision urged by the Council subsumes
a more abundant variety of readings: two readings are in-
creased to three, and the one-year cycle becomes a three-year
cycle. The readings are opened with a portion from the Old
Testament. The second is a New Testament reading from the
Epistles, Acts, or Book of Revelation. The third reading is from
one of the four Gospels. An effort has been made to correlate
the theme of the Old Testament and Gospel readings. In the
daily celebration of the Eucharist, a two-year sequential cycle
of readings from the Scriptures has been developed.

For the special seasons during the liturgical year, readings are selected from the Bible appropriate to each respective
occasion. As one proceeds through the Church year, the essential importance of the history of salvation through Jesus
Christ is stressed; it intends to re-enact the saving events of
his life (Advent and Christmas), death (Lent and Passiontide),
resurrection (Easter), glorification (Ascension), and the descent of the Spirit (Pentecost). This annual cycle is not a simple repetition, but as J. L. McKenzie points out, rather it is
oriented toward its eschatological fullness, thereby providing
hope for the future.[5] As a result of such a calendrical revision,
feasts like the rites of the saints are much reduced (n. 108).

The homily which is "highly esteemed as part of the liturgy itself" (n. 52) should "draw its content mainly from the
Scripture and liturgical sources. Its character should be that

of a proclamation of God's wonderful works in the history of salvation, that is, the mystery of Christ, which is ever more present and active within us, especially in the celebration of the liturgy" (n. 35). The homily should explain the meaning of the passage read from the Bible and should exhort the congregation to its devotional and practical applications. It can clarify the sequence of the biblical readings to the parishioners whose exposure to the Bible is often limited to the reading of it during the Sunday Mass.

As far as the divine Office is concerned, the Council also proposed a revision (nn. 88–101); according to this revision, Morning Prayer (Lauds) and Evening Prayer (Vespers) are emphasized, and the Office of Readings (Matins) may be recited at any hour of the day, though it retains its nocturnal character when celebrated in choir and should comprise fewer psalms so that other canticles from both the Old and New Testaments can be added. Mid-Morning (Terce), Mid-Day (Sext), and Mid-Afternoon Prayer (None) are maintained, while Prime is suppressed. To avoid monotony, the psalms are no longer to be recited within one week but over a four-week period of time. It was also recommended that there be a revision of the readings from the Bible so that more variety would occur and that well-selected portions from ecclesiastical writers and accounts of the saints be included in the Office of Readings.

The Ecumenical Movement

Finally, it must be pointed out that the Second Vatican Council distinguished itself through its paramount emphasis on the ideal of ecumenism. In fact, Pope John XXIII who initiated this Council was the first Roman Pope to pray with non-Catholic Christians. We read in the *Decree on Ecumenism,* n. 21, that despite many differences of views and beliefs between Catholics and other Christians, "in dialogue itself the sacred utterances are precious instruments in the mighty hand of God for attaining that unity which the Savior holds out to all men." This statement eloquently demonstrates the Council's herculean effort in search of true Christian unity.

The Council was sincerely convinced that the Bible should provide all believers of God with a basis for unity. The liturgical renewal in an ecumenical perspective should be predicated upon this very foundation. In fact, serious and fruitful dialogue is presently taking place among Catholics, Lutherans, and Anglicans.

When pure souls earnestly and humbly seek the divine will in the Bible, they, overcoming discords, can ultimately say in unison "Amen" before God.

Moreover, when biblical passages are read and expounded in the liturgy, God's message is being proclaimed not only to the faithful but also to the whole world.

QUESTIONS FOR DISCUSSION

1. Give biblical evidence for the close relationship between the Bible and worship.

2. What did the early Christians inherit from the Jewish worship service? In what way or ways were the Christians and Jewish services similar or different?

3. Why was the liturgical renewal felt necessary by the Second Vatican Council?

4. What impact has the biblical and liturgical renewal of the Second Vatican Council had upon the present relationship between the Catholic and Protestant churches?

5. Why should the Bible be used as an essential part of Church liturgy?

Notes

Introduction

1. According to the American Bible Society, 9,073,576 copies of the Bible were distributed in 1685 different languages during 1979. The 1979 Gallup survey reports that ninety-eight of one hundred contemporary American homes own at least one Bible.

2. This so-called "fundamentalist" assertion is not obsolete, but rather persistent, particularly because of the strong resurgence of evangelical Christians among Catholics, Protestants, and those outside the established churches. According to the 1979 Gallup survey, sixty-five million adults in the United States believe in the inerrancy of the Bible.

3. James Barr calls it "a classical model." See his *The Bible in the Modern World* (London: SCM, 1973) and his articles "Authority of Scripture" and "Revelation in History" in *The Interpreter's Dictionary of the Bible,* Supplementary Volume (Abingdon, 1976).

4. Cf. William Schneirla, "The Old Testament Canon and the So-Called Apocrypha," *St. Vladimir Seminary Quarterly,* Vol. 1, No. 3, New Series (1957), pp. 40–46.

PART I THE OLD TESTAMENT

Chapter 1

1. The majority of contemporary scholars still seem to hold such a positive view against the skepticism raised by some. For archaeological and tradition-historical problems concerning this period, cf. J. H. Hayes and J. M. Miller (eds.), *Israelite and Judaean History* (Westminster Press, 1977), pp. 70–148.

2. Cf. Claus Westermann, *The Promise to the Fathers: Studies on the Patriarchal Narratives,* tr. by D. E. Green (Fortress Press, 1980), p. 91.

3. Viktor Frankl, *Man's Search for Meaning,* tr. by I. Lasch (Touchstone Books, 1970).

Chapter 2

1. Cf. Gerhard von Rad, *Old Testament Theology,* tr. by D. M. G. Stalker (Harper & Brothers, 1962), Vol. 1, pp. 219–231.

2. Cf. H. W. Wolff, "The Kerygma of the Deuteronomic Historical Work," in *The Vitality of Old Testament Tradition,* eds. W. Brueggemann and H. W. Wolff (John Knox Press, 1976), pp. 83–100.

3. Cf. J. H. Hayes and J. M. Miller (eds.), *Israelite and Judaean History,* pp. 213–284.

Chapter 3

1. The archives from Mari, for example, attest to this fact. The prophetic movement in Mari seems to have many parallels to Israel's prophetic activity. Cf. H. B. Huffmon, "Prophecy in the Ancient Near East," in *The Interpreter's Dictionary of the Bible,* Supplementary Volume.

2. Cf. J. Lindblom, *Prophecy in Ancient Israel* (Fortress Press, 1962), Chapter III.

3. Abraham (Gen. 20:7) and Moses (Deut. 34:10) are called prophets. There is also a brief reference to a prophetic activity during the period of Israel's sojourn through the wilderness (Num. 11:24–29).

4. The prophecy of restoration at the end of the book (9:11–15) is an editorial addition in the post-exilic period.

5. These chapters provide us with no clear information as to whether she was a harlot or a cultic prostitute, or whether two different women were involved.

6. An emendation of the Hebrew text is needed here. *The Jerusalem Bible,* for example, has: "The believer shall not stumble."

7. Recent scholars, though not a consensus, hold that "the thirteenth year" of 1:2 refers to the year of his birth.

8. An explanation here of Ezekiel's understanding of the concept of "Israel" might be helpful. At his time, the northern country Israel (the northern section of the larger original Israel which had been composed of Judah to the south as well) had been destroyed. Then Ezekiel's hope of restoration was for the *whole* of Israel (the northern country and the southern Judah, undivided) which he considered to be the whole people of God.

Chapter 4

1. See S. Talmon, "Ezra and Nehemiah," in *The Interpreter's Dictionary of the Bible*, Supplementary Volume. Cf. also R. W. Klein, "Ezra and Nehemiah in Recent Studies," in *Magnalia Dei: Essays on the Bible and Archaeology in Memory of G. Ernest Wright*, ed. by F. M. Cross, Jr., *et al.* (Doubleday, 1976) pp. 370–372.

Chapter 5

1. Pius Drijvers, *The Psalms: Their Structure and Meaning* (Herder & Herder, 1965), p. 4.

2. Christoph Barth, *Introduction to the Psalms*, tr. by R. A. Wilson (Charles Scribner's Sons, 1966), p. 72.

3. Gerhard von Rad, *Wisdom in Israel* (Abingdon Press, 1972), p. 69.

4. *Ibid.*, p. 66.

5. J. A. Crenshaw, "Wisdom in the Old Testament" in *The Interpreter's Dictionary of the Bible*, Supplementary Volume.

Chapter 6

1. A well-known example from ancient time is Marcion (ca. 100–165), who rejected the Old Testament by insisting that Yahweh had nothing in common with the Father of Jesus. A modern vicious example would be the Nazi Germans.

2. Gerhard Hasel, *Old Testament Theology: Basic Issues in the Current Debate* (rev. ed.) (W. B. Eerdmans Publishing Co., 1975), pp. 125–127, itemizes the areas of relationship which follow.

PART II THE NEW TESTAMENT

Chapter 1

1. For this question, see S. G. F. Brandon, *Jesus and the Zealots* (Charles Scribner's Sons Co., 1967), pp. 208–220.

2. M. Kähler, *The So-Called Historical Jesus and the Historical Biblical Christ*, tr. by C. E. Braaten (Fortress Press, 1964), p. 80, n. 11.

3. G. Bornkamm, *Jesus of Nazareth*, tr. by Irene and Fraser McCluskey (Harper and Row, Publishers, 1960), p. 13.

4. See N. Perrin, *Rediscovering the Teaching of Jesus* (Harper and Row, Publishers, 1976) pp. 38–49.

Chapter 2

1. J. Jeremias, *New Testament Theology: The Proclamation of Jesus*, tr. by J. Bowden (Charles Scribner's Sons Co., 1971), p. 98.

2. *Ibid.,* pp. 61–68.

3. Sigmund Freud, *Moses and Monotheism,* tr. by K. Jones (Vintage Books, 1967).

4. E.g., Mary Daly, *Beyond God the Father: Toward a Philosophy of Women's Liberation* (Beacon Press, 1973).

5. Robert Hammerton-Kelly, *God the Father: Theology and Patriarchy in the Teaching of Jesus* (Fortress Press, 1979).

6. E. Schweizer, *The Good News According to Mark,* tr. by D. E. Green (John Knox Press, 1970), p. 385.

7. For a most recent example, see D. Juel, *An Introduction to New Testament Literature* (Abingdon Press, 1978), pp. 247–251.

8. See J. D. Kingsbury, "Form and Message of Matthew," *Interpretation,* Vol. XXIX (1975), pp. 13–23.

9. Cf. R. Pregeant, *Christology Beyond Dogma: Matthew's Christ in Process Hermeneutic* (Scholars Press, 1978), pp. 63–83.

10. A fundamental work on Luke's theology of salvation history is Hans Conzelmann, *The Theology of St. Luke* (Harper & Row, 1960).

11. Rudolf Bultmann, *Theology of the New Testament,* tr. by K. Grobel (Charles Scribner's Sons Co., 1955), Vol. 1, p. 76.

Chapter 3

1. Cf. E. Haenchen, *The Acts of the Apostles: A Commentary* (Westminster Press, 1971), pp. 81–90.

2. Paul also refers to such a council in Gal. 2:1–10. Despite some differences between them, there is broad agreement. For this question, cf. F. V. Filson, "Council of Jerusalem," in *The Interpreter's Dictionary of the Bible.*

3. Cf. F. F. Bruce, *Paul: Apostle of the Heart Set Free* (Eerdmans Publishing Company, 1977), pp. 441–455.

Chapter 4

1. K. Stendahl, *Paul Among Jews and Gentiles* (Fortress Press, 1976), pp. 7–23.

2. The words "I belong to Christ" in 1:12 are perhaps either a gloss or a mistake for "Crespos," the Christian ruler of the synagogue at Corinth (Acts 18:8; 1 Cor. 1:14).

3. Commentators often note that the city of Corinth was notorious for its licentiousness, which probably crept even into the Christian community there. But this information about Corinth most likely stemmed from malicious propaganda by its rival city, Athens. Corinth was morally neither better nor worse than other ancient Greek and Roman cities. Cf. H. Conzelmann, *Commentary on the*

First Epistle to the Corinthians, tr. by J. W. Leitch, *Hermetica* series (Fortress Press, 1975), p. 12.

4. Constance F. Parvey, "The Theology and Leadership of Women in the New Testament," in *Religion and Sexism: Image of Woman in the Jewish and Christian Traditions* ed. by R. R. Reuther (Simon & Schuster, 1974), p. 146.

5. For these different forms of love, see Paul Tillich, *Systematic Theology* (The University of Chicago Press, 1951), Vol. 1, pp. 280–282.

6. J. A. Hadfield, *Psychology and Moral: An Analysis of Character* (Robert M. McBride and Com., 1926), p. 82.

7. C. G. Jung, *Psychology and Religion: West and East: Collected Works,* tr. by R. F. C. Hull (London: Routledge, 1958), Vol. 11, p. 42.

Chapter 5

1. Cf. André Parrot, *The Temple of Jerusalem* (London: SCM, 1957) p. 87.

Appendix

1. This chapter by no means intends to present a thorough introduction to the liturgical tradition of Christianity. Rather, its focus is set upon the basic aspects of the question of the use of the Bible in Church worship in the West.

2. Dom Gregory Dix, *The Shape of the Liturgy* (London: Dacre Press, 1945), p. 38.

3. George Devine, *Liturgical Renewal: An Agonizing Reappraisal* (Alba House, 1973), p. 13.

4. This and the following quotations from the pronouncements of the Second Vatican Council are taken from *The Documents of Vatican II,* ed. by W. M. Abbott (Guild Press, 1966).

5. John L. McKenzie, "Roman Catholicism," in *Encyclopaedia Britannica,* 15th ed., Vol. 15, p. 996.